The
Sacred Grove

ESSAYS ON MUSEUMS

Dillon Ripley

SIMON AND SCHUSTER
New York

First printing

SBN 671-20317-7
Library of Congress Catalog Card Number: 76-79637
Designed by Edith Fowler
Manufactured in the United States of America
By H. Wolff, New York

*For the young museum viewers
Julie, Rosemary, Sylvia*

CONTENTS

INTRODUCTION

This book is a summary of my own impressions about museums. These impressions started filtering into my system through various senses, sight, smell, touch, through the pores if thermoregulatory processes involve a sense, at an early age. I assumed that what had been created or collected by other people was of great interest, not least if it gave some indication of how they lived and what they thought about. It seemed to me to be helpful to see the world of their time as these other people had reacted to it in the things they created. If I could learn something about this process, it might even be helpful to me personally. Fortunately or not, I never seemed to feel a generation gap in the sense of being alienated from looking at these testaments of the past. To me, even if older people seemed stupid or dull, I felt that they had at least lived before I was born and that they represented a magical sense of continuity, a hand reaching out from the instant past to the instant future, like Adam's hand in the Sistine Chapel.

Most people today who think about it accept the fact that everything in the cosmos, from heavenly bodies to ourselves, has developed, and, more important, continues to develop through evolutionary processes. Thus theoretical biology now pervades all of Western culture indirectly through the concept of progressive historical change. This has practical applications. We have a scientific basis for the ethical belief in the brotherhood of man. This is part of the chain of being and the continuity symbolized by Adam's graceful hand as painted by Michelangelo.

Culture is as badly described today as is ecology. Both derive, as words, from subjective approaches of our own selves. Culture stems historically from the increase in brain size of higher primates. Man and his culture evolved simultaneously through a complex series of interlocking, interreacting processes, which we now like to term feedbacks. Primitive forms of art, of religion and of science also played their part in affecting the development of neural processes and their integration in evolving man. New reaction patterns came with brain enlargement. Man adapts physiologically to his own culture.

What is almost certain in all this is that the various components of human culture are now required not only for the survival of man but also for his existential realization. Man created himself even as he created his culture and thereby became dependent on it.

I am sorry for young people who don't realize this and seek to escape, calling upon a generation gap. As Stanley Jolles recently said at a Congressional hearing, "rebellion without a cause, rejection without a program, and a refusal of what is without a vision of what should be" is, in fact, biologically impossible. One should merely blank out, leave the world in some form at this point. The instant we are born we are prisoners within our environment, within our living apparatus and within our culture. One cannot escape unless by more drastic measures than most young people are willing to contemplate. Nor would I advocate this for a moment. The voyage, while we are part of it, is much too fascinating. Take cultures, for example. Cultures vary between communities. They are as various as the degrees of separation between communities. It is almost certain that this will continue to be true for a long time. Then even to look at them, to observe them, is rewarding in itself. How can one be alienated from such diversity?

There is something about museums, I am convinced, which is of great importance for living if we can only understand and use it. Recently, at the Smithsonian, we had a colloquium on art teaching and art museums, as part of the opening in refurbished quarters of our National Collection of Fine Arts. Some of the panelists were depressing in their statements about museums: "Museums have become clubs and warehouses for the wealthy" or "We're great in this country for providing facilities and quarters for scholarship but very poor in providing scholars." It is true that there is only one chair in American art at an American university, and that in general art historians are considered to be beyond the fringe by "solid" history historians. Perhaps all this is part of what concerned another speaker: "Art museums and art education have failed to provide a literacy of the eye." And yet I believe, with still another speaker, that writers and other artists, including historians, can be taught by art and visual exercise: "Art is the literature of visual training."

So on the scholarly level we are missing something, and on the level of general education as well. People have still not found out how to use museums creatively for the betterment of us all, young and old. One of the maxims for the Smithsonian, which concerns itself with general research problems that have to do with museums, should be the importance of the study of two basic confrontations, the impact of man on his environment and the impact of the environment on man—and the effect that objects have upon man, and the influence that man has upon objects. Somewhere within these realms there are clues to our understanding of ourselves and, I suspect, our survival.

I am most grateful to my colleagues at the Smithsonian who have been helpful in discussions and thoughts on these subjects,

13

to Philip Ritterbush, Charles Blitzer and Frank Taylor with whom I have discoursed, and to Sidney Galler, Nathan Reingold and Sam Suratt. I am also in debt to friends at Yale University, particularly to G. Evelyn Hutchinson, and to the Editors of the Peabody Museum of Natural History, who have allowed me to reprint parts of my *Annual Reports* of 1961 and 1963 and to the editor of *Museum News* for permission to reprint part of an article published as "A Cabinet of Curiosities" in the issue of November 1961. Finally I am most indebted to Miss Adele Issa, who has painstakingly typed this manuscript.

The Sacred Grove

PREVIEW

The Collecting Instinct

I often wonder what makes people collect objects. Is there a reason in back of the urge to amass things? It is interesting to speculate on the origins of collecting, for a museum, quite beside its utility as a center for research and teaching, represents the fruit of a multitude of private collections.

A few summers ago my wife and I had an opportunity to observe two groups of people living in conditions which are popularly described as the Stone Age. A mountain valley, perhaps fifteen miles long, about 7,500 feet above sea level, cradled in the highest folds of the Nassau Range in the mountains of New Guinea, contains two groups of the Ndani and Uhunduni tribes, perhaps eight thousand souls in all.

In the past few years two families of American missionaries have arrived in the valley at the invitation of the tribes themselves. The tribal elders or headmen had come to this decision, so one missionary himself thought, in order to put a halt to the incessant wars and feud killings, which had reached a point beyond their endurance. The missionaries had directed the clearing of a small airstrip, and now the two families and two additional American nurses were ensconced in small, comfortable houses equipped with many characteristic American touches, all brought in piece by piece in single-motored light liaison planes. The Christian and Missionary Alliance and the Missionary Aviation Fellowship allowed the two of us and two

Ambonese assistants to fly up for a month's visit in this, the highest valley yet penetrated by the white man in what is now called West Irian, the western part of the island of New Guinea.

For the Ndani and Uhunduni, life is complex, full of ritual patterns. Men and women live apart in men's houses and women's houses. Men cultivate certain plants fraught with taboo such as taro, women certain others such as sweet potatoes. Their tools are sharpened wood stakes or spears, stone axes, knives, chisels and awls, and they are skillful with the bow and arrow. Wild game such as birds of over two hundred species and marsupial mammals, small wallabies, opossums (squirrellike creatures), rats, mice and the spiny echidna, relative of the Australian platypus, all are eaten whenever secured. Living so high in a damp cold climate, not far from frost, these Papuan tribes are at a bare subsistence level. The common term for this primitive stage of cultural evolution is the Stone Age. Domestic animals consist of the pig, which is not plentiful and is of great value, and a few dogs used for hunting. A number of chickens had been brought in by the missionaries.

Here, then, in this valley removed from the world, out of contact even with the sea which surrounds New Guinea, in touch only with the five or six neighboring valleys through trade or warfare, we found people of surprisingly different degrees of interest and intelligence. The men, self-consciously dominant, achieve their individual status by trade or warfare. Charged with these weighty matters and with the awesome responsibility of the taro crop, they feel that they have superior powers, that they are the supervisors and the arrangers of affairs. They are responsible for the health of the community. If that health is threatened, it is probably a woman who is at the bottom of it. Women obviously have strange, therefore magical, properties. Men must control them at all costs. Otherwise the male psyche might suffer. If a man dies other than in battle, it is obviously some woman's fault. She has "eaten his spirit," and the chances are it is some woman close to him, his wife or mother. Consequently, if a man dies, a woman is usually killed in revenge for his passing. One wealthy man who had ten wives had recently been very ill before we arrived in the valley. Two of the wives had been killed by his male relatives and the man had recovered. It seemed apparent to all that there was a connection between their death and his recovery. One or other of them had been "eating his spirit."

While the women make thread and tie head nets or with eyeless bone needles create handsomely decorated string or orchid-stem skirts, men endlessly rub rude chunks of hard basaltic rock with other stones to fashion huge ax heads or slim knives and chisels. These blades are sharp and highly efficient. More than that, they have individuality. The tactile sense becomes tremendously developed in people who are illiterate and skilled with their hands. The knives and the ax heads are as distinct and different as pieces of sculpture might be to us. The stones have identity. They are known, and the people who make them are known through them. Obviously, with time these stones and others of peculiar shape or color which are not carved but kept for reasons of choice are invested with a history all their own. They have a real identity, perhaps as much as books have with us.

These stones become collections. Certain important men have many stones. We call them headmen. They are not exactly chiefs, not necessarily members of a hereditary line, but they are prominent older men. Their words are weighty. They have amassed wealth or prestige as traders, although they are more prominent as burghers than as chivalric knights. These men have inherited some stones undoubtedly, but they also collect others. It was difficult to delve into this subject because the missionaries required the people to renounce not only weapons but also "fetishes" as they called them, in order to be baptized. Prior to visiting the valley I had imagined fetishes would be idols or graven images. But in this case the fetishes were stones. Consequently, by the time of our arrival the stones had been largely destroyed, thrown away, or burned in ceremonial fires. Steel ax heads and knives were being rapidly introduced as trade goods by the missionaries, and stone tools as such had already almost vanished. Here and there an old man could still be seen polishing a stone knife, but the art was already outmoded, a thing of the past.

But the past is not entirely foresworn. By talking with the people we discovered that the stones had not disappeared. Stone collections represent two things, religion and medicine. Certain stones, carefully wrapped up and secreted, usually buried in the ground, represent the spirits, the *manes*. Such stones are religious objects to be venerated. Possession means communion with the world of the ancestors from whom reassurance and a sort of spiritual strength can be derived. I will not quarrel with the missionaries, but from my own point of view I cannot see the harm in possessing these stones and also taking part in Christian worship. They did not seem like "fetishes" to me but more like an anchor to windward. To maintain a link with the past is to venerate the past and so to set down strong and useful roots which can maintain a culture through the twists and turns of fate. To order the destruction of the stones is to make these people *déracinés*. Some of the leaders felt this way, I think. One powerful headman, we were told, had kept his most venerated stone buried away out of sight, just in case the winds of fate brought by the missionaries should shift in the future and his kinfolk again need to take up a link with the past.*

* How wise he might be time alone will tell, for the Indonesian government has not been as encouraging to the missionaries as the former Dutch government. Should the missionaries leave, and the

The third sort of collection was what might be called an economic hoard. These were small yellowish cowrie shells, *Cypraea moneta*, "money cowries" as the common name is, which occur naturally in shallow water along the reefs of the seas of southeast Asia and Melanesia. Money cowries are traded up into the mountains from the seacoasts, passing from hand to hand, filtered gradually through many traders. The Ndanis have not seen the sea, nor have they seen the fishermen. The shells must be fifth- or sixth-hand by the time they come to these sequestered valleys. In spite of this, again by the tactile sense and by keen eyesight, these people have evolved a complex method of evaluating individual shells. Certain cowries have bumps or ridges along the margin of the shell. The quality and style of these bumps, as well as the size of the shell and its color—these several characteristics combine to create an elaborate scale of value. At the top, a single shell might conceivably be worth a wife or a pig. Fine shells in strings of thirty-two are usually sewn onto a strip of twisted woven bark cloth or kept in little groups or bundles in dried moth cocoons tufted with opossum fur, and wrapped securely in small plaited wallets of dried orchid stems. The little bags, like tobacco pouches, are objects of real beauty, beauty contrived to surround precious, rare and valuable things, *objets de vertu*. All such shells must first be enhanced by having the top filed off to reveal the inner cavity with its thin vaselike central columella. A certain tree sap is mashed into the surrounding space to achieve the best results.

These prepared shells graded in strings by their lumps and bumps are the real measure of a man's wealth. They form a sort of capital, like a private gold reserve. They are kept secreted

---

liaison planes as well, the tribes in these isolated valleys may well have to fall back again on their stones of all classes, including the stone axes.

and are brought out only on occasions of moment such as dicker-
ings over a bride, preparations for a great feast given to earn
prestige, for which a number of pigs may be needed, or war
settlements when damages or payments or fines may be levied.
In everyday trade they are virtually never used, as almost
everything is done according to an elaborate system of remem-
bered credit. If a man needed some potatoes at one time, he might
return tomatoes for them later, and so on and so on. This barter
system is especially brought into play while traveling. Remem-
bered debts of vegetables, salt or other foods serve as credit cards
of admittance to some relative's or friend's house in a neighboring valley. A seemingly intricate web of debits and credits must
be woven by every individual during his lifetime as he plays a
greater or lesser role in the life of his clan or tribe.

We brought a thousand shells into the valley with us, a thousand shells in a package, picked at random from the gleanings
of the off-island fishermen of Geelvink Bay. It was interesting
to learn how accurate was the Ndani and Uhunduni scale of
values. Of these thousand shells, not more than a few dozen
specimens had sufficient lumps and bumps on them to be of
much value. Only one had the bumps, the color and the size
to be of great value, worth an ax at least, perhaps a pig, or, if it
had been treated and filled with tree sap, perhaps a wife, who
knows? Another, smaller shell was too little to be of great value
but had the rugged contours to make it a significant shell. And
so from our hoard of a thousand shells, a random sampling, we
had one and a half shells of great value, some forty-five shells
of good value, perhaps another hundred of modest value, and
the rest were merely pennies, as it were. Without ever seeing
the sea or the source of supply, these mountain people had as-
sessed the cowries to reflect accurately the proportions of com-
monness or rarity in the character of the natural population of
common little shells. This inherent desire to collect is as highly

evolved as any professional coin or stamp collector could wish.

It seems certain that collecting is at least as old as culture. People such as these may collect for religious, medical or economic reasons, but skill and aesthetics enter at an early stage. The object acquired is centered in a decorative setting. The objects made have beauty, style and economy of line. The skills of craftsmanship evoke the sense of perception, jog the memory and interweave themselves in the very fabric of the culture itself. Culture, then, creates collections; collections create culture. A museum seems to represent the inheritance of one of the oldest instincts of mankind.

CHAPTER ONE

A Knock at the Door of the Muses

The word *mouseion* in Greek means a place or home for the Muses. Plato's Academy in the fourth century B.C. was a museum. Members of the Academy were organized as a *thiasos*, a sacred band, dedicated to the service of the Muses. As Rowell points out, "Speculation and research, particularly in mathematics, were the principal pursuit of the Academy and we can see in it the seeds of the organized institute of higher learning." [1]

Aristotle's Lyceum, even with its senior scholars, junior fellows, buildings and so forth, was a museum in effect, an institute of research, and so is the precursor of the famous museum in Alexandria. Founded by Ptolemy the First in the city laid out by Alexander in 332 B.C., that museum was a research institute, state-supported (*i.e.*, King-supported) with scholar members from all over the Greek world working together in association with the Library. This was the epitome of a research center, presumably with students and lectures, certainly with publications. Fields of study ranged from stylistics or critiques and research on existing manuscripts and texts to mathematics, astronomy and medicine. The Muses were venerated, and the institute then represented a *thiasos*. Its head was a priest appointed by the King.

At the same time as this development of the museum, as we should like to think of it, there were of course collections of art and treasures of various sorts, often associated with temples or other public buildings. These collections presumably were gathered to represent riches, to impress the visitors, and also to instruct and edify the tourist. It is worth remembering that these collections in themselves were not thought of as museums in the original Greek times. Not until the development of Rome as a great center was the dedication to the Muses associated with a collection or a treasure in itself. Rowell speculates that the cult of the Muses entered Rome shortly after 189 B.C. when the Roman General Fulvius returned from the conquest of King Pyrrhus' former capital of Ambracia in Epirus with over a thousand bronze and marble statues as well as a quantity of gold and silver. Fulvius built a temple in Rome to display this treasure hoard and dedicated it to Hercules of the Muses. The temple then became the forerunner of many similar temples dedicated to the Muses, places for self-gratification of the donor as well as for ritual, prayer and exhibition of treasures wrested from the Greek world, a world already synonymous with glories and wonders of the past.

Eventually the center of Rome became a museum in itself, a place of display for the plundered objects of beauty of an earlier time, for a series of pictorial representations of historical events; and, in the Forum of Augustus, was a hall of fame, a series of statues of the creators of Rome from Aeneas on down. At the height of Imperial Rome everything was decorated with treasures, from the Forum to the baths to the private villas of the rich. Display and ostentation reached a point where they became a coveted way of life. But peripherally, as always, this achieved some benefit. Taste, at least, was created and elevated in the process. People could love Greek art for itself and were not in the process debased. In the exposure to beautiful objects, in the acquiring of taste, some good follows from the original evil embodied in the ruthless act of pillage. So it seems to have been in history. Man continually covets and in the process destroys, and so eventually acquires. In the ensuing time, other generations acquire taste, only to collect, to enjoy beauty and then eventually to attract covetousness again.

Certainly Rome in its heyday must have looked like a mixture of New York's Hall of Fame, an outdoor sculpture garden, two or three large art museums called temples, shrines here and there, and of course the Coliseum, an earlier Shea Stadium, all combined. There are places today that are as florid and flushed as the Forum—witness the sculpture galleries of the United States Capitol or the monuments to glory of Mussolini's time.

But what happened then to the sacred band? We seem to lose track of the main thread, the original purpose. Perhaps not really, for with the triumph of Christianity in Europe, churches began to take on many of the habiliments of the sacred band. The Church became the center of intellectual life as well as the collector of treasures. The early museums were inextricably linked to the evolution of the Church as a stabilizer in uncertain times of violence, as a communicator of tradition and culture, of art and aesthetics, of philosophy and a sense of beauty and taste. The concept of the great art collections of medieval times originated in and from the Church and spread, through its influence as a creator of taste, into the princely families, first of Italy, then of neighboring countries. By the late fifteenth century there was again a public art collection in Rome, thanks to Pope Sixtus IV.

At the same time libraries, if they existed, were of and related to the Church. Monks and priests, along with exceptional laymen, early humanists and poets or scientists, were the descendants of the sacred band, trained as they were in some way through Church-related schools or libraries.

Somewhere along the way then there began to be a first division between the collection as a collection and the collection associated with the worship of the Muses, the Platonic ideal of speculation and research. In fact, of course, the concept of Plato's Academy still exists in some of the disciplines of study which involve collections. But in the public mind the museum today is the outgrowth of the private cabinet of curiosities.

And what was the "cabinet"? The cabinet and its related terms implied a hoard or collection of rarities of some sort. Pictures, for example, were said to be collected or held in a gallery or *pinacotheca*, from the Greek—a room for paintings or sculpture. A chamber or closet or cabinet was used in Western Europe to describe a place where rarities were kept and into which the connoisseur could retire for private contemplation. Storehouse is another term, in the sense that Dr. Johnson thought of a museum as a repository of objects which could thus be preserved. The great private collections of Jean, Duc de Berry, and the Medicis were kept in protected places of storage called *guardaropas*.

Much of this collecting instinct develops into the set of themes which both enhance and denigrate the word museum. As Wittlin says; "The following qualities, both spiritual and material, seem to be inherent in them" (*i.e.*, the terms by which museums were described in the sixteenth, seventeenth and eighteenth centuries): "interest in learning and encyclopaedic approach to inquiry; inspirational values; privacy and secrecy; rarity; boastful costliness; features connected with storage accommodation and with the hiding of things."[2]

If Wittlin is right, as I think she is, in saying that these themes remain as residual measures in people's minds, then it is no wonder that the public museum of later times has suffered from this mixture of attitudes, most of them so far removed from the Platonic ideal.

Francis Taylor is thinking of this same overriding problem of definition when he says: "If the term 'museum' strikes terror

27

to the heart of the average layman, it is as nothing compared with the sense of panic which its sound produces in the poor innocents who spend their lives rationalizing its very existence. Going back into the far reaches of time, the word 'museum' has succeeded in meaning nothing vital to anyone in particular, yet at the same time it has strangely meant all things to all men. Through a metamorphosis lasting many centuries it has emerged from the simple designation of a temple of the Muse to be the encompassing catch basin for all those disparate elements of hereditary culture which are not yet woven into the general educational fabric of modern society. And since education has been defined [by whom, I wonder?] as the 'art of casting artificial pearls before real swine,' it is only natural that museum workers should have concerned themselves with the elaborate furnishings of the trough at the expense of the digestive capacity of the feeders." [3]

Francis Taylor is, of course, speaking of the public museum of today, and its theme of display, but the purposes of these cabinets were not always thus. The cabinet afforded an opportunity for encyclopaedic studies. Many of the great collectors were also great teachers. The Bologna physician Ulysses Aldrovandus was a sixteenth-century scholar who, in the spirit of true learning, was an encyclopaedic man, what we today, in this age of specialty, might term a Renaissance man. Teaching cabinets, both in science and art, continued through the eighteenth century. Harvard University had a Repository of Curiosities which unfortunately burned down in the 1760s. Here, in these cabinets, was implied a collection as an enhancement of knowledge, something which instructs and elevates through a wide or indeed a complete circle of knowledge.

At the same time the state treasures or church treasures continued to grow, to be collected avidly and with covetousness. Here are the continuing themes which tantalize anyone looking for the meaning of the word museum. The royal cabinet of the Electors of Saxony in Dresden was obviously an art gallery. Seventeenth- and eighteenth-century cabinets continued to be amassed by extremely wealthy persons, sometimes eccentrics among whom collecting had become a sort of mania. English travelers going abroad on a grand tour (but of course these were privileged people who would carry letters of introduction) were urged to visit some of the famous cabinets. Among these were Signor Rugini's at Venice, Valentini's at Giessen, or that of Bruckmann at Wolfenbüttel. Partly because of its trade with the Far East (which brought back curiosities in its ships as well as wealth to its citizens), Amsterdam became a center for "closets." There were the famous collections of Swammerdam (also a great scientist), of Albert Seba, and of Frederik Ruysch, the anatomist. The latter gentlemen were both visited by Peter the Great of Russia, that inquiring modern, who eventually bought their collections, whereupon both set about amassing further collections. On these tours collections were bought, if possible, and art dealers and brokers of antiquities became common. The Paludanus collection was bought by a German Duke, and many of the Italian collections ended up by purchase in Austria, Spain or England.

Voyages and travel helped to spark the growth of collections. The seventeenth century also saw the birth of the academies of science, groups of savants and letter writers who banded themselves into elite societies in Italy, England, France and Germany from 1657 on. However, neither the collectors nor the societies were concerned with disseminating their knowledge to the world at large. One of the only collections which had at all a public flavor is that of John Tradescant and his son, John, at South Lambeth in London. The younger John published a catalogue of the collections in 1656, which listed many benefactors who had presented objects, including King Charles himself, but still the collection remained open only to the invited. As the poet Flaxman complained:

Thus John Tradeskin [sic] *starves our greedy eyes
By boxing up his new found Rarities.*

And what rarities these were, a veritable *omnium gatherum.* There was a "Dodar" (Dodo) from the island of Mauritius—this, the only known specimen of a giant extinct flightless pigeon, perished when burned at Oxford nearly a hundred years later. There were also beasts and fishes, shells, insects, serpents, fossils, minerals, exotic or "Outlandish Fruits from both the Indies, with Seeds, Gummes, Roots, Woods, and divers Ingredients Medicinall, and for the Art of Drying," including Brazilian herbs and medicines such as cinchona bark.

There were huge collections of coins and medals as well as all sorts of oddities—artistic, archaeological or ethnological. All these objects later came to Elias Ashmole and were presented along with his own collections to Oxford University to form the genesis of the great Ashmolean Museum. Thus, by 1682, there was the first University museum, one whose collections would be available for scholars and for public instruction.

The Ashmolean was a beginning, but a slender one. Collectors were still of the private variety, and philanthropy as far as museums were concerned was unknown. One of the greatest eighteenth-century collectors was Margaret Cavendish Holles Harley, Duchess of Portland (1714–1785). Her most famous purchase was the vase now known as the Portland Vase. Horace Walpole, a friend of the Duchess, spent some three hundred pounds on purchases at the sale of her collection, and also wrote an account of the numerous objects she had collected. The document is now among the Walpole papers in the (Farming-

30

ton, Connecticut) collection of Mr. Wilmarth Lewis. This is
what Walpole writes of the Vase:

> For the three or four last years of her life She checked
> her purchases (it is like trying to control a vice!); but some
> few months before her Death She was tempted by the cele-
> brated Barberini Vase, imported by the noted Virtuoso
> (savant collector) Sr. William Hamilton, Minister at
> Naples, who had purchased it and the head of Jupiter Sera-
> pis in Basaltes, of Byers a Ciecone (guide and presumably
> dealer) at Rome. The Princess of Palestina, Mother of
> Prince Barberini, had during her Son's Minority, to pay
> her gaming debts, sold these Curiosities to Byers for 500
> pounds and Byers had resold them to Sr. William, as it was
> also said for 1000 pounds. The Duchess gave 2000 pounds
> to Sr. William for them, a fine cameo of Augustus, and a
> fragment of an Intaglia of a Hercules.

When the Duchess died her collection was sold, by her order,
except for gifts to her children and grandchildren. The auction
brought £. 10,965 10s. 6d. The Portland Museum still contained
the Portland Vase, and the passion for collection shown by
members of her family continued for several generations.[4]

A spectacular eighteenth-century museum was that of Sir
Ashton Lever. Lever was a country gentleman who lived near
Manchester. He was born in 1729 and went up to Oxford to
Corpus Christi College. His first collections were of live birds,
and eventually his aviary at Alkrington Hall was said to be the
best in the Kingdom. In 1760 he began purchasing shells, and
from this went on to fossils, stuffed birds, savage costumes,
weapons and every kind of curiosity. Finally the collection began to spill out of Alkrington Hall, and in 1774 Lever decided

31

to open a public museum in London. Here he charged admission, to reimburse himself and to pay for the running of the institution. His charging of admission must have been also an attempt to reduce the number of visitors, for he inserted a notice in the newspapers on September 13, 1773, as follows:

This is to inform the Publick that being tired out with the insolence of the common People, who I have hitherto indulged with a sight of my museum (at Alkrington), I am now come to the resolution of refusing admittance to the lower class except they come provided with a ticket from some Gentleman or Lady of my acquaintance. And I hereby authorize every friend of mine to give a ticket to any orderly Man to bring in eleven Persons, besides himself whose behaviour he must be answerable for, according to the directions he will receive before they are admitted. They will not be admitted during the time of Gentlemen and Ladies being in the Museum. If it happens to be inconvenient when they bring their ticket, they must submit to go back and come some other day, admittance in the morning *only* from eight o'clock till twelve.

s./ "Ashton Lever."

It would be hard indeed to behave this way today, when museum directors tend to vie with each other for ever larger and larger public attendance. Lever succeeded in renting Leicester House in London, where at first his museum became an immensely successful fashionable resort. An entry from Mme. d'Arblay's diary reads:

Tuesday, December 31st. I went this morning with my dear father to Sir Jn Ashton Lever's, where we could not but be entertained. Sir Ashton came and talked to us a good deal. He may be an admirable natural*ist*, but I think if in other matters you leave the *ist* out you will not much wrong him. He looks full sixty years old, yet he had dressed not only two young men, but himself, in a green jacket, a round hat, with green feathers, a bundle of arrows under one arm, and a bow in the other, and thus accoutred as a forester he pranced about, while the younger fools, who were in the same garb, kept running to and fro in the garden, carefully contriving to shoot at some mark, just as any of the company appeared at any of the windows.

Sir Ashton evidently had become something of a showman with Carnaby Street overtones. In an earlier letter from Susan Burney to her sister, Mme. d'Arblay, dated 16 July, 1778, Susan writes:

Saturday morning we spent extremely well at Sir Ashton Lever's Museum. I wish I was a good Natural Historian, that I might give you some idea of our entertainment in seeing birds, beasts, shells, fossils etc. but I can scarce remember a dozen names of the thousand I heard that were new to me. The birds of paradise, and the humming-birds, were I think, among the most beautiful. There are several pelicans, flamingos, peacocks (one quite white) a penguin. Among the beasts a hippopotamus (sea horse) of an immense size, an elephant, a tyger from the Tower, a Greenland bear and its cub—a wolf—two or three leopards—an Otaheite dog (a very coarse ugly-looking creature)—a camelion—a young crocodile—a roomful of monkeys— one of them presents the company with an Italian song— another is reading a book [are these alive perhaps?]—another the most horrid of all, is put in the attitude of Venus de Medicis, and is scarce fit to be looked at. Lizzards, bats,

33

toads, frogs, scorpions and other filthy creatures in abundance. There were a great many things from Otaheite [probably from Captain Cook's voyage]—the complete dress of a Chinese Mandarine, made of blue and brown sattin—of an African Prince. A suit of armor that they say belonged to Oliver Cromwell—the Dress worn in Charles 1st's time etc. etc.

Eventually Lever's Museum became less fashionable and he lost money. His attempt to have Parliament buy it for the nation failed (a tragedy, considering how enormously valuable much of the material would have been today), and it was eventually sold off by lottery. The natural history collections, including the types of many species first made known to science by Latham and other contemporary naturalists, have disappeared from view. Lever himself died not long after the museum failed, and his fame vanished with him, though Gilbert White, the Vicar of Selbourne, wrote: "Over Leicester-house gate should be written in letters of gold *Museum Leveriense!*" High praise indeed from the shy Vicar.

In the meantime another and even greater collector created by his will the first and greatest public museum of natural history. Sir Hans Sloane, the celebrated physician, president of the College of Physicians and of the Royal Society, had collected voraciously throughout his whole life, both by voyages (to Jamaica) and by purchase (most important was the Charleton or Courten collection). By 1733 Sloane's collection, including just about everything from coins and pictures to fossils and pathological specimens, numbered above 69,000 items. His library alone contained 40,000 manuscripts. He estimated that his collections were worth more than 80,000 pounds. In his will, Sloane humbly requested Parliament to reimburse his heirs to the tune of 20,000 pounds, one quarter of the value, so that these things "tending many ways to the manifestation of the glory of God, the improvement of the arts and sciences, and benefit of mankind, may remain together . . . and that chiefly in and about the city of London, where they may, by the great confluence of people, be of most use." Sloane's admirable wish was heeded; in 1753 Parliament appropriated the money; in 1759 the British Museum, the greatest of its kind in the world, was opened to the public.

Of course, the British Museum as we know it today did not spring forth fully accoutered. In 1786 a visitor complained that except for "some fishes in a small apartment which are begun to be classed, nothing is in order, everything is out of place; and this assemblage appears rather an immense magazine, in which things have been thrown at random, than a scientific collection, destined to instruct and honour a great nation."

The New World entered the field of museums at about this time. The first museum as such began in Charleston, South Carolina, with the Library Society of that city, which set up an exhibit and collections based on the natural history of South Carolina in 1773. Not long after, Charles Willson Peale, the portrait painter of Philadelphia, who had come to know many of the most prominent figures of the Revolutionary War and had painted their portraits, began an exhibition of his own in his painting room in Philadelphia, his first important specimen being the bones of a mammoth dug up in New York State. From his atelier the collections were moved into the new hall of the American Philosophical Society in 1794 and finally in 1802 to the upper floor of Independence Hall. Peale's collections were on public exhibit and for many years, during the active life of Charles Willson, were financially successful. Later, under his son Rubens, they dwindled in importance as a money-maker, and finally became incorporated into the scientific research collections of the Philadelphia Academy of Natural Sciences.

Another son of Charles Willson, Rembrandt Peale, also a painter, is distinguished for having built the first American museum in Baltimore, in 1813. This building, which still exists and is now the Municipal Museum of the City of Baltimore, was designed in the style of a neoclassical English town house of large dimensions. There was a huge "drawing room" on the second floor and two very large rooms at the back. The upper floor had portraits; on the lower floor were "Birds, Beasts, Fishes, Snakes, Antiquities, Indian Dresses, and War Instruments, Shells and Miscellaneous Curiosities." In a small side room, for an additional twenty-five cents, the visitor could see:

THE GRECIAN BEAUTY
A Statue of Wax, from head to foot, colored Like Life—and the picture of

THE DREAM OF LOVE
Both efforts of art, intended to display the
beauty, softness, symmetry and grace of
the female form . . .

The War of 1812, stock-market trouble, heavy debts and mortgages prevented Rembrandt Peale from realizing his dream. He eventually sold out to his brother Rubens, and by 1830, the collections having been moved, the building was purchased for a city hall.

The early museums in the United States suffered from the relatively straitened resources of the former colonies at the time. Patrons or collectors, *virtuosi*, as they were called, were few. Philanthropy hardly existed, although Benjamin Franklin, along with his thrift, heartily approved of it. Rembrandt complained of the wealthy merchants of Baltimore who "in the midst of business . . . are strangers to the social virtues."

In Europe, meanwhile, national pride and the national conscience combined to rescue many private collections which gradually found their way into the hodge-podge galleries of Copenhagen, Uppsala, Paris and St. Petersburg. The nineteenth century saw the development of national galleries and museums in most European countries, followed by the Americas and the east. The new liberal ideas of that century, the new interest in history, the development of scientific principles in inquiry affecting historical studies, the history of art, and finally, in science, the great development of evolutionary thought and the discoveries in geology and paleontology—all of this tended to focus interest on museums. Museums became centers for national pride, for research into the past and for public instruction. They began to become again homes for the Muses as scholarship was deemed an essential component of the whole. The problem of what has happened to solve the paradox of collections and collectors, on the one hand, and research and scholarship on the other is perhaps still for the future. Can museums live up to their Platonic founding ideals without killing off the collectors or sinking under the weight of materials? Can museums collect dead things and remain alive? Not only does it seem to me as if they can, but also that in so doing museums can find the seeds of a part of our salvation.

CHAPTER TWO

A Glance at the Nineteenth Century

The nineteenth century is the epoch of the rise of the public museums. It is also the period during which museums first created that public impression which has been so disheartening in subsequent years to museophiles. The word museum, instead of seeming to imply a center of learning, came to mean something ponderous, dull, musty, dead, a graveyard of old bones of the past.

In France the Louvre, in Spain the Prado, in Italy the Vatican, these museums were palaces, so heavily ornamented and decorated that it was difficult to see the objects. Museums such as these and other former private collections were hard to get into, and if the public did arrive, they were likely to find a cluttered mass of curiosities, arranged, if any arrangement existed, for the cognoscenti. The theory, of course, of this new age of liberal thought was that the former private collections were now to be open to all for public education and enlightenment. But in fact the collections continued to be administered as if they were private. Regulations made them difficult of access, and the jumble and lack of arrangement made the exhibits often unintelligible. The tradition of grandeur persisted. Marble, vast vistas, high, pedimented ceilings, gilding and decoration assumed that these were indeed noblemen's palaces only just vacated, and that the public was admitted on sufferance, as it were.

As Wittlin points out, these were hardly the surroundings in which to inspire the spirit of learning and enjoyment. Rather they tended to awe or perhaps even antagonize the visitor. She quotes the French poet Edmond de Goncourt as saying, "It is my will that the objects of art which have contributed to my happiness should not be buried in the cold grave of a museum."

Museums could be as cold and uninviting, even though said to be established for the public good, as any other panacea for the edification of the soul, such as cold baths before breakfast or enforced doses of castor oil. It might be said in answer to the query Why should a town have a museum at all?: "Because a museum and a free library are as necessary for the mental and moral health of the citizens as good sanitary arrangements, water supply and street lighting are for their physical health and comfort." [5] But this did not imply that the medicine would be palatable. The jumble and disorder was fascinating in itself, but fatiguing, I suspect, to the average viewer. Greenwood speaks of a "Chinese lady's boot encircled by a necklace made of shark's teeth, next to the stuffed relics of a dog." Thomas Barbour[6] speaks of the old-time museum man as being a miser who could never throw anything out. As he says:

Any object no matter how revolting or loathsome, seen sufficiently often, blunts the senses, and one becomes disinclined to the effort necessary to destroy it or get rid of it.

Pride of possession is a curious attribute of mankind. This was brought sharply to my mind recently when it occurred to me to ask myself, "Why didn't Mrs. Chase *give* the Peabody Museum her gallstones?" Many other people had, for there were a pint or more of miscellaneous gallstones in the Peabody Museum in Salem, curiously enough in the case with an old reindeer. But these were donated gallstones; it was only Mrs. Chase's that were on loan. The

answer is, Mrs. Chase's gallstones were larger than any
others in the whole place and she obviously just couldn't
bear to part with them permanently. . . . Not long ago I
was [reminded of this] reading the last *Annual Report of
the Curator of the Museum of the Royal College of Sur-
geons* in London. This venerable institution, containing
much material that was priceless indeed, suffered a direct
hit from a German bomb. It was almost completely destroyed and the story of the catastrophe was told, sadly and
meticulously, by its distinguished curator. . . . Along with
the many terrific [valuable] losses suffered by that venerable institution were listed the facts that the jar containing
Napoleon's bowels was cracked and that the rib of Robert
the Bruce was broken.

My own childhood memories of the Litchfield Historical Society included a combination of a Victorian armchair, some
early ladies' clothes, an assortment of farm implements and a
glass case containing the forequarters and head of an African
lion resting in the grass.

Usually, just in back of these sorts of collections was the storage area, some parts of which are termed by Barbour "Glory
Holes." Antiquarian and curatorial instincts often go hand in
hand, and an almighty jumble of detritus can be the result.
Barbour again:

When I first took charge of the Agassiz Museum, I found
one big glass jar filled with chicken heads, another with
burned matches, another with old rubbers. The chicken
heads were potential material for dissection, and the fact
that a dollar's worth of heads filled a twenty-dollar jar
never occurred to the man who ate those chickens, who was
no other than Louis Agassiz himself.

The two great European museums that influenced the course of museum-making in the nineteenth century were the British Museum and the Louvre. Both were in palaces, the British Museum in the house of the Duke of Montague, built in the style of a French chateau of the seventeenth century with a grand staircase and elaborate murals in the French taste. In the entrance hall was a statue of Shakespeare, ornaments from a Hindu temple and the skeleton of a hippopotamus. On an upper floor were artificial curiosities and artifacts of "uncivilized" tribes and nations. By 1808 the fourteen rooms were organized as:

1. Ethnographical curiosities
2. Harleian curiosities, mummies and ancient weapons (the Harleian collection followed the great natural history collections of Sir Hans Sloane as a gift to the nation)
3. Lansdowne collection with many copies and casts of works of art
4. Manuscripts
5–6. Portraits of famous persons
7. Royal library with portraits of kings of England
8. Banqueting Room
9–14. Natural History

Later the Elgin marbles were added, as well as the treasures of Assyria and Halicarnassus. In addition there were Egyptian collections from the savants attached to Bonaparte's army who had surrendered them to British forces in 1802. All of this was arranged with great difficulty as collections piled up, and was viewed by visitors on four days of the week, Monday through Thursday. Persons wishing to see the collections were to arrive in the anteroom between eleven and twelve o'clock, and only one hundred twenty a day were allowed in, provided each person's credentials had been examined and entered in a visitor's book. On certain Fridays there were special tours. Those who had finally gained admittance were allowed in in guided tours of up to fifteen at a time, as is still done in certain palaces or monuments today. As can be imagined, most visitors were whisked rapidly through the rooms, and it is said that the guides often ignored questions put by the visitors, or were misinformed themselves. Little of this seemed destined to bring out the best in the average visitor, or indeed in the custodians themselves.

In Paris the Louvre was opened to the public after the Revolution, in 1793. It was available for visitors on three days of one "decade," the Republican unit replacing the week. A commission was formed known as the Conservatoire de Muséum National and charged with the arrangements of the galleries. However, the conquests of Napoleon Bonaparte included the shipment of endless trophies and art treasures. By 1807 a new rotunda was opened and a guidebook published on art trophies captured by the *Grande Armée* in the campaigns of 1806–7.

Of course, later, the Congress of Vienna in 1815 had to deal with this accretion. The rightful owners pressed for the return of their paintings and art treasures, and the harried curators, who had spent so much time arranging everything, lost most of their collections. M. Denon, the director-general, whose industry and care for the collections make him perhaps a model of an art-gallery director, was so horrified by the arrival of the foreign commissioners to reclaim their works that he persisted in taking pictures out of the carts on which they had been loaded and carrying them back himself to try to replace them on the walls. Finally Denon, realizing the inevitable, cried out in the manner of a Minister of Culture of today, "Let them take them! But they lack eyes to see and France will always show her superiority in the arts; for her masterpieces were always better than those of others!"

In the years to follow, succeeding collections made their appearance and transformed the Louvre once more into one of the leading museums of the world. Egyptian and Assyrian antiquities were followed by Louis Philippe's collection of Spanish paintings, and by 1848 the museum was declared national property.

As these two great museums developed, it was inevitable that their influence should be felt in the New World. But whereas the European prototypes were created in former palaces, most of the great museums of this country and Canada arose from private benefaction or philanthropy, and that during the past hundred years. Many of these collections represented a conscious effort by what was called the enlightened class to donate materials for public show in order to elevate and educate our citizens. Art collections and products of nature alike were to be exhibited for public edification. The William Corcorans, the Peter Coopers, the George Peabodys of the time were concerned, as a moral issue, with the educational and cultural development of their fellow citizens. Benefaction, philanthropy, were not only virtues; there was a strong, a zealous missionary desire to uplift, to create cultural equality as one of the fundamental outgrowths of our new democracy. All of our citizens should have the same opportunity to imbibe culture, to understand the arts, to develop familiarity with science, as part of their heritage as inheritors of the new lands. This theme seems to have run through the founding motives of the institutions in this country and to have been reflected in the Land Grant Act and the setting up by state governments of state colleges. Today of course it continues to be part and parcel of our government concern with the arts and humanities no less than with the sciences. And, of course, as private philanthropy declines proportionally in these days, government becomes increasingly invested with the social consciousness reserved for enlightened individual benefactors of the second half of the nineteenth century.

As Francis Taylor describes it, the American Museum "is an

43

American phenomenon, developed by the people, for the people, and of the people. . . . It is significant that in the original program of the organizing committee of the Metropolitan Museum of Art, dated January 4, 1870, it was stated that the purpose of the association was to afford 'to our whole people free and ample means for innocent and refined enjoyment, and also supplying the best facilities for practical instruction and for the cultivation of pure taste in all matters connected with the arts.' " And, as he says, this is indeed the fundamental philosophy of American art museums, quaint as the phrasing may sound today.

This is in the spirit of the muses. However, the greatest development during the nineteenth century of the true spirit of museums came in the area of the sciences. Here, better than in any other area, were collected the ingredients out of which research, teaching and scholarship evolved. The time was ripe. Eighteenth-century voyages of discovery had helped to set the stage for research. The wonders of the world of natural history, which had already electrified the savants of the late eighteenth century, had brought forth the labors of Carolus Linnaeus, the Swedish biologist, whose permanent and monumental contribution was the encyclopaedic notion of putting order into the natural products of the earth in the form of a system of nomenclature. Systematic order, once grasped as possible, developed the keenest interest among scientists of the time, who proceeded to arrange minerals, plants and animals into trees of life, and to relate them one to another. By the early years of the century, succeeding scientific voyagers like Humboldt and Bates, Hodgson and Hooker, not only trained scientists but also enthusiastic amateurs were sending back materials for the emerging public museums as well as for the cabinets or laboratories like the Jardin des Plantes in Paris, home of such preeminent scientists of the time as Cuvier and St. Hilaire. Out of these efforts a notion of teach-

ing as well as research developed. The two concepts were insepa-
rable in the evolving scientific tradition.

In the New World, Peale's public cabinet evolved into the
privately initiated Academy of Natural Sciences in Philadelphia,
founded in 1812, whose learned and philanthropic supporters
made it one of the outstanding world scientific institutions by
the 1840s. In 1812 another society was founded which had great
influence at the time. This was the American Antiquarian Society of Worcester, Massachusetts, whose museum has recently
been described in a delightful essay by Shipton.[7] Speaking of the
librarian (and curator), Samuel Foster Haven, he quotes him
as referring to the visiting public as "a crowd of careless people
. . . regardless of admonition, and intent only on the gratification of curiosity." As Haven put it, the Society was "intended
for scientific use and gratification of enlightened curiosity" not
"a mere museum of articles for idle and unprofitable inspection." The traditions of the Philadelphia Academy and the
Worcester Society were those of scholarship.

By 1848, when Louis Agassiz, the great Swiss naturalist, came
to Cambridge to take the professorship of zoology and geology in
the Lawrence Scientific School of Harvard College, the mood of
inquiry and scientific museum organization was sufficiently
established that in ten years Agassiz was able to persuade Harvard College to set up the Museum of Comparative Zoology as
a separate department of the college. As a scientific impresario
and creator of *faites accomplis*, Agassiz was matchless, and the
Harvard Corporation, urged on by the Massachusetts State leg-
islators and prominent private figures in Boston's business
circles, all of them under the Agassiz spell, seemed powerless to
prevent the creation of his persistent dream. The Museum,
founded in 1859, the year of publication of Charles Darwin's
Origin of Species, has had a continuing seminal influence on the

45

development of American science. Louis Agassiz became the Museum's first director and by the end of the fourteen years of his life devoted to it, there was an impressive building, superb research collections, and, more importantly, the great teacher had trained many of the leading natural scientists of the country. Although Agassiz, for essentially theocratic reasons, was unable to accept Darwin's theories—unlike his friend Asa Gray—his students and his successors indeed went on to make Harvard's Museum a center of evolutionary thought. His son, Alexander Agassiz, who as a young man had traveled west and made a fortune, came back and took over the Museum and its financial perils, running and financing it as a kindly and benevolent despot for over thirty years. The traditions established by the Agassiz family were devotion to scholarship and research, and about them gathered a formidable coterie of geologists, paleontologists and animal biologists.

Other colleges were also involved with museum practices of a contemporary nature. College collections of objects existed in every older institution, but not all of them had the luck to find the combination of initiative and philanthropy represented at Harvard. Yale was virtually as lucky in the presence of Professor Benjamin Silliman and his son-in-law, Professor James Dwight Dana. Silliman the elder, whose son, Benjamin the younger, succeeded him as Professor of Chemistry, had the good fortune to develop an interest in geology and mineralogy, and in the course of his labors to begin to attract collections as well as students to New Haven. Silliman began his own scientific career in 1802 at Yale upon being appointed Professor of Chemistry and Natural History at the age of twenty-three. I say began, because he had been training for the law.

Realizing the need for firm foundations, he traveled to Philadelphia to consult with one of the scholars who later founded

46

the Academy of Natural Sciences, Dr. Adam Seybert, from whom he learned mineralogy, and commenced his travels in search of materials for the Yale cabinet and collections. In the course of his correspondence he developed a friendship with George Gibbs, a wealthy collector of Newport, Rhode Island, and finally persuaded popular subscribers, as well as Yale College, to find the necessary money to purchase this collection in 1825. The Gibbs cabinet of mineral specimens, the best of its kind in the country at the time, formed the nucleus of the Yale scientific collections and in a sense initiated the need for a museum. That museum became a reality with the advent of O. C. Marsh, a young scientist by inclination who graduated in 1860 from Yale, where he studied geology under Dana and chemistry under B. Silliman the younger, and who thereupon resolved to undertake graduate study in New Haven at the Sheffield Scientific School, and also in Germany. His success was so pronounced that in 1866 he became Professor of Paleontology at Yale, the first person to be appointed to such a post in the New World.

Marsh was not only an outstanding personality, an energetic field man and a splendid research scientist, but he also had a maternal uncle, George Peabody, whose beneficence had seen Marsh through college. George Peabody was a banker, originally from Danvers, Massachusetts, long established in London, who was America's paramount philanthropist of his time. With the urgings of his mentors, Dana and the Sillimans, the young Professor Marsh had little difficulty in stimulating his bachelor uncle into an act of generosity directed at Yale College. George Peabody had already given the Essex Institute, in Salem, Massachusetts, funds for its financial salvation (and rapid rechristening as the Essex Institute *and* Peabody Museum of Salem). He had created the Peabody Homes in London. His munificence to Danvers had produced a spontaneous rechristening of the town

47

as Peabody, and on his return to his natal place, the inhabitants joyfully unhitched the horses pulling his carriage and pulled it by hand through the streets.

In 1866, three months after Marsh's appointment as Professor of Paleontology, and after four years of mulling over the subject, George Peabody decided to give Yale College the sum of $150,000 for a Museum of Natural History. Thus began the Peabody Museum, whose collections made by Marsh and his zoology colleague Verrill, a pupil of Agassiz, formed the real foundations of geology and zoology at that university. Nearly half of all subsequent degrees of Doctor of Science or Philosophy taken in geology at Yale have been obtained by men who worked on the museum collections and have gone on in subsequent years to head the geological surveys of the nation, Federal and state, as well as to teach at the leading universities.

It is said that the trustees of Harvard College, amazed at a Massachusetts man's munificent gesture to Yale, pulled successfully at Mr. Peabody's coattails and reminded him of their college. Whatever the cause of Mr. Peabody's concern, he matched his gift to Yale with a like one to Harvard in the same year to start a museum for archaeology and ethnology (the Peabody), which has developed as a leading center for scholarship, particularly in the archaeology of Middle America.

These college museums, and others like them at Princeton, Amherst College and the University of Michigan, equaled the activities of the private societies springing up in cities all over the country as centers for lectures, research study laboratories and teaching. Some of the small natural history societies developed into large city museums like the Academy in Philadelphia and the Milwaukee Public Museum, which started as a city museum in 1882. The greatest of the city museums is the American Museum of Natural History, founded in 1869 and dedicated to research and public instruction. The organization of this museum (along with the Art Museum, eventually the Metropolitan) created a landmark in civic-trustee relations. Under the charter, eventually ratified by the City of New York and the state, the partnership principle emerged; the city would erect a building and provide funds for maintenance, the trustees would own the collections and seek funds for the staff of "investigators" and public lecturers. The last decades of the nineteenth century saw the American Museum of Natural History grow, especially under the tutelage of its third President, Morris K. Jesup, into the most effective instrument for the public interpretation of the collected materials of science in the nation. Whereas the smaller university museums, working at the training of students, produced a fine synthesis between research and teaching at the highest levels of scholarship, the American Museum in New York personified the growth of a public institution which utilized its research staff, graduates of the university museums, not only to study the collections, but also to begin a long and arduous process of interpretation for the public. Here displays and exhibits for the public evoked the principle of "public instruction."

By contrast, few of the university museums could afford to concern themselves with public exhibits. In fact, in some museums, such as Harvard's, they made a fetish of distaste for exhibits, which in its origins perhaps traces back to the days of the eighteenth-century cognoscenti. A pure research institution "had no time" for the instruction of the layman (shades of Sir Ashton Lever's "common people")! The public science museums were no less capable of employing distinguished research curators. However, they were more conscious of civic and public support, therefore public obligations, and also closer to trustee boards, who concerned themselves with the interplay between the collections and the people, hence the exhibits. In all of this the American Museum's influence was paramount—an innovative theme in exhibit preparation ran through its whole developing history. Under the influence of Professor Bickmore, who gave public lectures on natural history, as well as J. B. Holder and J. A. Allen, all pupils or associates of Louis Agassiz, an important scientific program was established. In exhibits, the pioneer efforts of Mrs. Mogridge, Frank Chapman, Louis Fuertes, and later, Carl Akeley, produced the first great diorama exhibits, relating to the public the environmental surroundings of animals in a convincingly effective manner for the first time in North America.

The great art museums of the nineteenth century were to develop more slowly and with less convincing evidences of learning. The impetus was more Roman than Greek, more temples adorned with trophies than groups of *thiasos*, the sacred band. A few museums encouraged teaching. The Pennsylvania Academy of Art, founded at Philadelphia in 1805, embodied the spirit of the eighteenth-century patricians like Charles Lennox, Duke of Richmond, who opened his gallery and house in 1758 as a free school of art for poor students. The academy tradition has persisted to this day in Philadelphia. It was embodied as well in Peter Cooper's will setting up the Cooper Union School, with its collections of objects for study and instruction in art, in New York in 1859. W. W. Corcoran, whose philanthropy created the original Corcoran Art Museum in 1874 in Washington, had a somewhat similar idea, for it was assumed that eventually art instruction would be part of the whole design for the gallery.

Far fewer of these art galleries were associated with organized instruction in colleges. The first of these was the Trumbull Gallery at Yale, built as a museum to house Jonathan Trumbull's paintings in 1832, and now the Yale University Art Gallery. Mr. and Mrs. Trumbull were buried beneath the floor of the original gallery as a condition of the bequest and have moved twice, for the original building was given up as an art gallery in 1868 and the present building dates from 1928, with a major wing added in the 1950s. This first gallery was unrelated to teaching as such, and historically it has been Harvard's Fogg Museum of Art which has had primacy of place in the early training of art historians in this country.*

All of these science and art museums and the related fields of history and anthropology began to show the signs, which became so evident in the twentieth century, of division of goals, of cross-purposes. Which came first, the scholar or the collections? And where did the collector fit in? If a scholar, not a collector, wished to work at his research with collections, would he be welcome? What were the collections for? Research, aesthetic appeal, as documents in the history of the earth or of man's culture, or for personal display or civic pride? With the development of museums as great public institutions there came a sense of muzziness about their purpose. This has bedeviled the inhabitants of museums ever since.

* The first museum training program seems to have been a curatorial course introduced at the Pennsylvania Museum and School of Art in 1908.

CHAPTER THREE

The Smithsonian in the Nineteenth Century: A Microcosm of Museum Problems

The dilemma of the rise of a great nineteenth-century museum is graphically illustrated in part of the development of the Smithsonian Institution. Founded finally by a somewhat reluctant United States Congress after eleven years of bickering over the purposes of the unexpected bequest of James Smithson, the Institution's subsequent growth under its first two Secretaries, Professors Henry and Baird, had somewhat the character of Dr. Doolittle's fabulous beast, the pushmepullyou. (Some of the early history of the Smithsonian, and what little is known of the life of James Smithson, was well told by Oehser in 1949,[8] and again, recently, by Hellman in 1967). [9]

Joseph Henry, who was perhaps the best-known scientist of his time in the United States, had conceived a general plan of operation for the Institution. On this his acceptance of the post of its first Secretary was based. On the basis of his interpretation of the mysterious benefactor's enigmatic phrase of instruction, "for the increase and diffusion of knowledge among men," Henry's consistent plan was composed. In accordance with the "Will of Smithson," Henry wrote:

To Increase Knowledge. It is proposed—
1. To stimulate men of talent to make original re-

searches, by offering suitable rewards for memoirs containing new truths; and,

2. To appropriate annually a portion of the income for particular researches, under the direction of suitable persons.

To Diffuse Knowledge. It is proposed—

1. To publish a series of periodical reports on the progress of the different branches of knowledge; and,

2. To publish occasionally separate treatises on subjects of general interest.[10]

The details of this plan were not only submitted to the Board of Regents of the Institution and approved by them (in 1847), but also to a number of scientific and literary societies where the program won universal approval. Henry thus had every right to expect that the Institution's purposes as an advanced research center would be understood, and would be capable of widening knowledge for the benefit of mankind. As he pointed out, "The Government of the United States is merely a trustee to carry out the design of the testator." He did acknowledge, of course, that the act of Congress establishing the Institution required that a library, a museum, and a gallery of art should be included in the design of the physical facilities. In this connection the Board of Regents resolved to divide the income of the Institution ($30,-910.14 in 1855) into two equal parts; one to undertake publications and research as outlined above, the other to pay for library, and museum and art gallery acquisitions. As Henry noted, these divisions were by no means incompatible (although the amount of money was too small by far even in 1855). As he reported, "A library will be required, consisting, 1st, of a complete collection of the transactions and proceedings of all the learned societies in the world; 2nd, of the more important current periodical publications, and other works necessary in preparing the periodical reports." In addition the Institution should make "special collections, particularly of objects to illustrate and verify its own publications," and "also, a collection of instruments of research in all branches of experimental science."

Henry felt that library catalogues of other libraries were of major importance for the Smithsonian library, as well as other materials, in order to make the Institution a great bibliographic center that would attract students. He felt that natural history collections would arrive under their own momentum without having to use precious purchase funds, and in many ways he was right. As Coleman pointed out, "The government became an ally of museums as the army, and to some extent the navy, got into exploring." [11] From the Wilkes Expedition collections of 1842, down through the Pacific Railroad Surveys of 1855 and subsequent years, through various State surveys, some of them dating as late as the WPA days of the 1930s, the Smithsonian's U. S. National Museum has received, and often has farmed out to other museums, a tremendous amount of freely acquired material.

As far as art was concerned, Henry was all for it. "Attempts should be made to procure for the gallery of art, casts of the most celebrated articles of ancient and modern sculpture. The arts may be encouraged by providing a room, free of expense, for the exhibition of the objects of the Art-Union and other similar societies." The latter project, which has survived in principle down to this day, although meritorious and public-spirited, has often been a sore subject with curators and exhibitors alike. But Henry was anxious to develop art collections. He was greatly taken with the Elgin marbles. In a little notebook of his *circa* 1848, Joseph Henry writes;

> In 1847 I visited London and in company with Professor
> Bache made some attempts to procure for this country a set

of copies of the Elgin marbles. We were together one day in the British Museum when our attention was attracted by a number of men engaged in taking casts of some of the larger of the Elgin marbles. We asked for whom these were intended and were informed for a present to some foreign court. We asked why we could not get a set for our own government, the answer was that nothing would be easier all that was necessary would be to interest our Minister and a word from him would be sufficient. Mr. ———, our Minister, was not however impressed with the matter and declined to do anything.

Subsequent intercessions with Mr. N. Biddle, "then in the zenith of his influence," as well as J. C. Spencer, Secretary of the Treasury, "who called a Cabinet council"—all failed. So ended an effort at cultural exchange.

An important additional point made by the Professor was that "distinguished individuals should also be invited to give lectures on subjects of general interest." It seemed best to try to give courses of lectures on special subjects rather than to cover a whole topic in one lecture. Sometimes, however, a single lecture on some literary subject, or on the life of a distinguished individual, or the history of a discovery sufficed. These were very popular and the best of them were digested and reprinted in the *Annual Reports*. The nineteenth century was the era of lectures, personified by the Lowell Institute in Boston and the Atheneum in Richmond, and Henry managed to secure a tremendous variety of eminent personages as lecturers. It was planned that these should be given mostly when Congress was in session in order to afford an opportunity for members of the Congress to have illustrated to them new discoveries in science and new objects of art.

I wonder how many of the perennially busy members of the

Congress managed to get to these learned occasions? Perhaps the Professor had as little luck as he seems to have had with the special committee of the House of Representatives to whom his plan of organization and operations had been referred in 1855. As Henry reported, "The committee of the House had not time, before the close of the session, to visit the Institution, or to make such an examination of the management and the condition of its affairs as the importance of the matter referred to them would seem to demand."

In any case the lectures in any one year varied from "Grandeur and Fall of the French Bourbon Monarchy" and "History of the War Between Russia and Turkey" to "Vegetation," educational movements, China, electricity and the nature and cure of the bite of serpents. Lecturers ranged from men like the Sillimans, father and son, of Yale, and Professors Agassiz and Gray of Harvard, to Mark Hopkins, the President of Williams College, George P. Marsh, whilom Minister to the Sublime Porte—as the Sultanate of Turkey was known—and on to a miscellany of Alexanders from New Jersey, Channings from Massachusetts and Devereuxs from New York.

Joseph Henry's plans for the Institution were naturally dependent to a considerable degree on his choice of colleagues. The first and most important appointment made by him was that of Charles C. Jewett, named Assistant Secretary and Librarian in 1847, at the request of certain of the Regents who were determined to see the creation of a great national library under the aegis of the Smithsonian. The second was Spencer F. Baird, appointed Assistant Secretary for Publications, Exchanges and Natural History in 1850. Both were men of extraordinary ability and character. The library plans of Henry and Jewett seemed to coincide perfectly well at first. By 1853 Jewett, already a noted authority on libraries, was able to convene in New York the first international conference of librarians ever held. Jewett was president of the conference, and among the resolutions passed at the meeting was one endorsing his far-reaching proposals for a central national catalogue of library holdings by book title. His plan, far ahead of its time, was eventually adopted in principle by the Library of Congress. It was a remarkable advance, and the pity was that Professor Jewett was perhaps too impatient for immediate results. His library at the Smithsonian remained of necessity small. Henry rightly questioned its becoming a major univeral library, especially in what we would term the humanities, and recommended patience and fiscal austerity. Finally the men came to a parting of the ways, and the Smithsonian lost the most innovative librarian of his time.

In spite of the departure of Professor Jewett, the Smithsonian library by 1865 had become so crowded that Joseph Henry suggested that most of the books be deposited in the Library of Congress. The great increase in holdings was partly due to the admirable cultural exchange system worked out with foreign libraries and institutes as well as individuals, which gave the Smithsonian a steady and increasing volume of presentation and exchange serials and monographs. The matter at the time was most seriously considered and finally passed as a bill by Congress in 1866. Dr. Gill, then Smithsonian librarian, was transferred to the Library of Congress as an assistant librarian in charge of the Smithsonian deposit. As Adler said, "From this time on the Institution became, in a certain way, an office for receipt and record of publications. Exchanges were continued, but there was no other source of increase, while the entire care of the books was assumed by the Library of Congress." [12]

For better or worse, a change of direction had occurred. The Smithsonian lost one of its tripod legs of research. Techniques of research in bibliography, in iconography and in library study which might well have continued to make the Institution a pioneer in a much-needed field, were given up. The emphasis

57

began to shift in a small but significant way toward pure science on the one hand and museum stewardship on the other. In this last category Professor Baird was preeminent. Probably the most influential museum scientist of his time after Agassiz, Baird was first and last a museum collector, a man who left no stone unturned to amass collections for the U. S. National Museum—in Thomas Barbour's pithy phrase, "a pack rat."

The Nation's Cabinet of Curiosities so-called, the National Institute, housed in the U. S. Patent Office, was the original National Museum, which, having fallen on hard times as the collections increased, was judged to be the responsibility of the new Smithsonian. However, as noted earlier, Professor Henry, while accepting the idea of a museum, seems to have been more convinced, as time went on, that the slender funds of the private endowment should not be encumbered in administering the Government's collections. As he said, "the Smithsonian Institution will readily take the supervision of an establishment of this kind, and give plans for its organization and arrangement, provided it be requested to do so, and the means [the necessary money] for effecting the object be liberally supplied."

The arrival of Baird from Carlisle, Pennsylvania, complete with freight cars containing his own personal collections of bird skins and skeletons, eggs and nests, reptiles, fishes, amphibians and fossils, should have indicated that, in the sense at least of being a collector's collector, here was another sort of Agassiz. In ten years he had perfected a system of developing exchanges, stimulating government and private collectors and outfitting expeditions.

"No bride ever devoted more thought and attention to her trousseau than did my father to the fitting out of each of these explorers," wrote his daughter, Lucy Baird.

As Hellman has noted, the lists of donations accepted by Baird for the Museum do not suggest that the Institution in those days had any medium for rejection—no rejection slips had been printed up. Such miscellanea were accepted as "Sealed Bottles Containing Water from the Dead Sea, Chicken with Four Legs, Insects from Catlett's, Va., Three Fish-Hooks from Thomas Day, Keeper of Seguin Light," implying a certain lack of discrimination. In 1858 the collections at the Patent Office, the old "Cabinet," were formally transferred to the Smithsonian, and in 1861 the Smithsonian bureau of the U. S. National Museum was formally instituted. Congress had been appropriating funds for the Institute all along, and these were transferred to be annually appropriated to the Smithsonian in 1858.

In order to exhibit the collections properly cases were set up and a formal museum setting was created. Baird, in a famous letter to the Honorable George P. Marsh in 1853, had expressed some of his philosophy as a collector and museum administrator:

"You ask who is to describe nondescripts and what is to be done with the things when they come in. That is not my particular business now; my duty is to see that no chances are lost of advancing science, leaving the future to take care of itself. And indeed I expect the accumulation of a mass of matter thus collected (which the Institution cannot or will not 'curate' efficiently) to have the effect of forcing our government into establishing a [separate] National Museum, of which (let me whisper it) *I* hope to be director. Still even if this argument don't weigh now, it will one of these days, and I am content to wait."

In effect, Baird did better for himself. He succeeded Henry as the second Secretary of an Institution which had incorporated his museum and which has been heavily involved in museum custodianship ever since. Baird's greatest coup came in 1876 with the Philadelphia Centennial Exhibition. In connection with the Federal Government's participation, the Smithsonian was involved in the preparation of five exhibits, partly in cooperation with the Fish Commission and the Indian Bureau of the Department of the Interior. These had to do with "Smithsonian Activities—Animal Resources—Fisheries—Mineral Resources—and Anthropology." In the plans for the Centennial it was quite clearly anticipated that a large number of exhibits would be left in the hands of the National Museum, and indeed this is what eventually happened. The exhibits of some thirty-four foreign governments as well as numerous states eventually descended on the Smithsonian in seventy-eight freight cars, including the things collected by Baird and his colleagues themselves. Some of Professor Henry's worst housekeeping fears must have been realized. A new building was essential. The original Tuscan castle was already crammed. As Henry wrote: "These questions [of space] will involve another—whether it is advisable to continue, at least without some modification, the connection which now exists between the Smithsonian Institution and the National Museum.

"The Museum is destined to an extension far beyond its present magnitude. It is an object of much interest to all who visit the National Capital, and is of great value as exhibiting the natural resources of the country, as well as a means of public education."

Again there is the feeling of a branching of interests, a certain dichotomy.

However much Professor Henry may have been concerned with his own research, his own interest in physics, and however parsimonious he may have felt in husbanding the slender income of the Smithson bequest and the slim allowances of Congressional appropriations, it can never be said that he was not broadly interested in science or failed to recognize the importance of museums. As a scientist he was not only broad but eminently sensible. Although so close to Agassiz, he nevertheless incisively took the other side in the dispute on Darwin's new theory on evolution, among the earliest American men of science to do so. In 1864 he wrote to Asa Gray: "I have given the subject of evolution much thought, and have come to the conclusion that it is the best working hypothesis which you naturalists have got. It, in fact, gives you the first basis or real scientific foundation to stand upon which you have ever had."

It is worth noting his prophetic words as a museum administrator at the laying of the cornerstone of the American Museum of Natural History building in June, 1874 (here appear echoes of his original plan as well as premonitions for the future):

> Modern civilization tends to congregate the population of countries into large cities . . . cities tend to increase more rapidly than the general population . . . [due to] the education of the working classes and the introduction of labor-saving machines . . . cities in proportion to their extent and rapidity of growth engender habits of thought and of action of a character the reverse of progress and which, if unrestrained, would tend to disintegrate society and resolve it into its primitive barbarous elements. . . . These principles are eminently applicable in New York."

> It is therefore of the first importance that those who possess the intelligence, the influence, and the power, who from the experience of the past are impressed with the tendencies as to the future, should endeavor to provide all the means possible to avert evils similar to those with which this city has been afflicted, and which tend to afflict it in a still greater degree in the future.

His prescriptions included liberal support for religious activities to neutralize the selfishness engendered by the fierceness of human competition in a city, and in addition support for museums of art and of nature which can supply intellectual pleasure and instruction. The museum of natural history-to-be can be a temple of nature. And what is Henry's temple? A temple of the muses. Collections in themselves, though valuable, are still wanting an essential element. In Henry's view the museum must have a professor who can give free lectures on the objects, on phenomena of nature, on the mysterious principles of life, on geology and the history of man's own evolution. He went on to speculate on the impact on New York City of another Agassiz, the lecturer par excellence, the man of wisdom at the zenith of his instructional powers.

The final leg of the tripod of Henry's museum, to make the temple complete, is to be his "college of discoverers," men capable not only of "expounding established truths but of interrogating nature and of discovering new facts, new phenomena, and new principles."

In Joseph Henry's view, then, a museum could indeed be a *thiasos*. Speaking of the Smithsonian he says that after twenty-five years of incessant effort the directors had at last persuaded Congress that this was the design of the Smithson bequest, and that the whole energy of the establishment should be devoted to "the advance of science." Henry's "first class scientist," like the poet a discoverer, is probably born, not made, is "liberally provided with means," with research tools and space, and is of course protected from the pressures or controls of public life by being in the "college," the museum.

Meanwhile the objects kept on pouring in. Fortunately Congress passed a bill in 1879 to give the Smithsonian $250,000 for an exposition building to house the overflow of exhibits. By this time, too, Professor Henry was dead, and the new Secretary, Baird, and his assistant, Dr. George Brown Goode, set about the arrangement of the exhibits which were said to be a wonder of their time, exciting admiration here and abroad. Goode, who unfortunately died prematurely at the age of forty-five, was undoubtedly a preeminent museum man. His plan for the new museum opened in 1881 was sound and advanced; the collections should in effect be *records* of scientific knowledge; the aims of the museum should be to make its contents serve as a stimulus to *research*, and lastly, by illustrating through exhibits, not only materials but the manifestation of man's thought and activity upon them, the museum should be for *education*.

But while Baird was a supreme administrator, a superb cataloguer and a meticulous collector, he seemed to be preoccupied with statistics, with the collecting of collections themselves, with the omnium-gatherum as a be-all and an end-all in itself. Perhaps the changes in the spirit of the *Annual Reports* signified a trend. As Hellman has noted, although Baird started a new taxonomic series, the *Proceedings of the United States National Museum*, he cut down on the publications for original research. The *Annual Reports* themselves became somewhat pedestrian. Plans for research were omitted or condensed. Notable events, such as the various special lectures or papers on different aspects of original research produced during a year, tended to be slurred over or omitted. Instead, by the 1880s the *Annual Report* itself became a catalogue, with its multiple curiosa in the form of acquisitions faithfully listed. The public image of the "Nation's Attic" was beginning to emerge.

In spite of this pedantic impression, a certain measure and balance persisted. Baird and his wife acted as hosts to men of science in somewhat the tradition of the Henrys. Younger, unmarried scientists or visitors, geologists, ethnologists and biologists lived as well as worked in the rooms of the Smithsonian building in the upper floors or towers. There is no doubt that the research aspects of the Institution continued, although the tone seems more muted. However, one of Baird's strong points in the decades of the sixties and early seventies was his support of expeditions. His influence as what today would be called a science administrator continued to increase. Called to testify before

Senate Committees, acting as advisor to Secretaries of State and the military, Professor Baird cut a notable figure in the promotion of Government interest in science. Perhaps his lasting memorial has been in the work he organized on fisheries and marine resources, precursors of the Government's present interest in oceanography and the biology of the sea.

Finally, in terms of research it should be said that Baird helped in the formation of the Bureau of Ethnology of the Smithsonian, the pioneer organization devoted to ethnology and linguistics in this country. This bureau had its origin in the first work of the Smithsonian, expeditions and publications relating to Indian archaeology and languages. It received its coordinating impetus from Major John Wesley Powell, the one-armed Civil War veteran, who in May 1869 started off on his third summer exploration, financed by a Federal grant to the Smithsonian. His jumping-off point was where the just-completed tracks of the Union Pacific Railroad crossed the Green River in southwestern Wyoming. This was the epoch-making first descent of the Colorado River. Powell became famous overnight. The resulting Congressional interest in his explorations as well as his activities in making known the ways and customs of the vanishing Indian tribes assured the success of the Bureau, which was officially founded under the Smithsonian in 1879 and of which he continued as Director until his death in 1902. Powell, in the multifaceted manner of the time, turned out to be a geologist and a pioneer in land use as well, and doubled as Director of the Department of the Interior's U. S. Geological Survey from 1881 until 1894.

It is difficult to overestimate the influence of the Bureau of American Ethnology on the whole history of American anthropology. As Professor Claude Levi-Strauss testified in his remarks in 1965 at the Bicentennial Celebrations of Smithson's birth, no set of books had more affected his studies as a young man than the volumes of the Bureau of American Ethnology. His first savings as a student were used to attempt to acquire a set for his own library. These publications have formed a living testimonial to Henry's plan to commemorate Smithson's name with research and publication. This was how the Professor urged his millionaire audience in New York in 1874 to believe, to do likewise, to create New York's own "College of Discoverers." Smithson's name is "a household word in every part of the civilized world," and as memorials, "what, in comparison to this, are local monuments, pyramids of flint, statues of brass or obelisks of marble"; echoes all—by comparison, echoes of "Ozymandias, king of kings."

Some of the millionaires at least reacted, although in different ways and somewhat later. Perhaps the Rockefeller Institute and the Carnegie Institution of Washington of the following years epitomized Henry's "College of Discoverers."

Baird died in office in 1887 and was succeeded, not by George Brown Goode, who had helped set up the new exhibits, but by Samuel Pierpont Langley, an astronomer and professor of physics at Western University at Pittsburgh. Self-taught, Langley had had a brilliant career as a young astronomer-inventor; he had perfected telescopes of his own, invented the bolometer and a flying machine. Langley was a research scientist and thus personified one aspect at least of Henry's tradition, but my own impression is that he did not relate museum activities with research and teaching in the manner of his predecessors. Except for the promotion of the zoo as an early form of conservation education, and except for his fondness for children, for whom he set up a children's room in the museum, he seems to have been dedicated primarily to his own brand of research.

The great apparent tragedy for the Smithsonian at this stage was the death, in 1896, of Goode, the one administrator in the Institution who had seemed to grasp the essential need of combining the recording and documenting function of museum collections with original research and with public education. In his death at the age of forty-five the museums of the country lost a champion, the man whose *Principles of Museum Administration*, published in 1895, lived on as a standard for more than fifty years.

By the turn of the century, Langley was, at sixty-six, already rather an old man, withdrawn in his laboratory round which the grass was kept at knee height to discourage strangers. He was not to retire, however, but to continue as Secretary until his death seven years later. A certain sense of direction and, above all, a sense of élan, of flair, seemed to have departed from the Institution. There was a museum, a research laboratory and a zoo. There was, of course, the eternal public too. But the men involved seemed mostly to want to be left alone.

CHAPTER FOUR

Museums in the
First Half of the Twentieth Century

The paradox of museums continues apace down to the present day. As Joseph Henry had stated it, "The tendency of an Institution in which collections form a prominent object, is constantly towards a stationary condition: with a given income, the time must inevitably come when the expenditures necessary to accommodate the articles with house room and attendance will just equal the receipts," and, warming to the subject, "There is indeed no plan by which the funds of the Institution may be more inefficiently expended, than that of filling a costly building with an indiscriminate collection of objects of curiosity, and giving these in charge to a set of inactive curators." [13]

Through the latter part of the nineteenth century and the early part of this one museums seem to have drifted into two positions which gradually became separate, almost polarized. On the one hand certain museums came to exist purely as storehouses, as catch-alls, elegant as they might have been. The average historical society was a good, though often inelegant, example.

"Send grandmother's dresses there," said the desperate descendant as an alternative to sending everything to the public dump heap. "Maybe someone will cherish them."

Many art galleries in our cities suffered the same fate. Either the curator hoped for more and better quality in future by being nice to the Joneses in their hour of need or he simply didn't know how to say no. Paintings and decorative objects poured in, usually without a coherent plan, and the common attic-for-all image was the result.

Science museums have had more luck in this respect. The miscellaneous rocks or butterflies, fruit of last year's nature class, have had a way of getting disposed of, and in general only material collected by expeditions or on organized field trips has been commonly retained.

But all museums have suffered from this image. By the mid-twentieth century the Smithsonian Institution itself had come to be thought of not as a sponsor of basic research, but as the "Nation's Attic." The Institution has somehow never received the credit that was its due. As Washburn said in his essay on Henry quoted above:

"By providing positive support to scholarly activity at a time when the universities were largely uninterested, [Joseph] Henry may have provided an all-important example and alternative which forced the more rapid evolution of this trend [toward research] in the somnolent centers of undergraduate instruction."

The other attitude, the contrast to the attic or genteel storehouse, was that a museum was indeed a practicing laboratory or an educational center. Indeed, the American Association of Museums coined the ringing phrase "the people's university." This contrasting attitude, while bravely maintained in a few institutions, continued to receive a diminishing measure of attention from the public as well as from scholars. The rise of university research automatically downgraded the role of the independent institution.

Certainly by the second decade of this century museums had developed into a far more limited set of centers, attic-like or not, than the promise of the nineteenth century seems to have foretold. In the sciences, laboratory and experimental research in

68

biology, chemistry and physics, especially under the impetus of the new teaching laboratories in western Europe, came to be the focal interest in the universities. In biology the developmentalists, working with a few simple laboratory animals, and largely trained in German universities, came to play the dominant role. Biomedicine and the birth of the massively supported campaigns against human disease attracted many of the foremost brains into physiology, embryology, genetics and organic chemistry. The school of descriptive biology became a byway except insofar as the needs of economic botany or medical research may have had peripheral concerns.

The school of evolutionary studies was to emerge only gradually, largely through the work of geologists or paleontologists at first, men like Henry Fairfield Osborn, W. D. Matthew, and later W. K. Gregory, who helped to create a bridge between the university and the museum. The American Museum of Natural History in New York pioneered in developing an understanding of the role a twentieth-century curator could play in university and teaching relations. It was that great institution which maintained a living link between its own paleontological curators and the faculty of Columbia University, so that during this transitional period of neglect there could still exist a viable relationship. Curators in New York's museum were first equated to faculty appointments at Columbia, not walled off, incarcerated in monasteries, as they had begun to be elsewhere. This was already an accomplishment, a reversal of the pendulum which had swung so dangerously away from recognition of the basic research role of a curator. Another museum which succeeded in developing a close university relationship was that at Berkeley —the Museum of Vertebrate Zoology, which, as a developing department of the University of California, was able to inaugurate a whole school of ecological studies under Joseph Grinnell.

Only a hundred years before, as Conant has pointed out, "the colleges viewed their professors primarily as teachers rather than as research men." [14] Again quoting the farsighted Joseph Henry in 1846 on the subject:

"We have in the United States upwards of a hundred colleges each one of which has a corps of Professors in the line of science and yet scarcely any one of them makes an attempt to enlarge the bounds of human knowledge. The truth is we are over-run in this country with charlatanism; our newspapers are filled with the puffs of quackery and every man who can burn phosphorous in oxygen and exhibit a few experiments to a class of young ladies is called a man of Science."

In geology, with its strong right arm of paleontology, this trend never seriously developed. The theoretical evolutionary work of paleontology continued to exert a powerful fascination on younger men. The field stayed open, as it were, available to new minds of a later day, who could draw upon the evidence slowly being brought to light by the zoogeographers and geneticists about the plasticity of the evolutionary material of animals and plants, genes and chromosomes, under conditions of geographical isolation. In oil geology, too, a whole new field of applied research based on museum collections began to develop, dependent on the identification of microfossils and brought into prominence by Professor Schuchert of Yale, his collections and his pupils.

In anthropology as well, the value of records of vanishing cultures, preserved largely through the efforts of museums or museum-related bureaus such as the Bureau of American Ethnology at the Smithsonian, was always fully realized. The bridge between museum anthropologists and university anthropologists remained open, and has remained open thanks to the pioneering work of Krober, of Boas and his school and of the great university-sponsored museums of anthropology at Harvard, Pennsylvania and Michigan. There has never really been a pronounced coolness between scholars working in anthropology in museums and those in universities.

Indeed, I am persuaded that museum training in anthropology is still vital, and that a social anthropologist of the stature of Margaret Mead, for example, could not have arisen outside of the context of a museum. But it is a truism that museum-based anthropology has declined in importance since the end of World War I, except for a brief flurry of applied interest in knowing about faraway places which came to the fore during World War II. The plain fact of the matter is that most anthropological museum collections of ethnographic material more than fifty years old are of relatively little interest except to connoisseurs or as typological examples. Largely collected in haphazard fashion, these old collections of striking or decorative objects tend to be preserved *con amore*, with little related supporting data. The modern ethnographer cannot tell the *meaning* of a Solomon Islands food vessel unless perchance he has been to the Solomon Islands or unless someone else of equal skill has, and, in the process, has lived with the owners, heard the chants, observed the rituals, and has discovered the magic significance of that particular piece of ritual or liturgy with which the bowl was associated. In many of these primitive cultures, enameled tin cups may already have replaced the old hand-hewn bowls with their special magic before ever the tale was told. The remaining old men who could describe a vanishing culture or reveal an all but unspoken language have died or are about to die.

The great storehouse concept of museum keeping was gradually refined over the last years of the nineteenth century. The consummate achievement of this concept has been the creation of the great *gallerias* of our day, the art museums. The great art museums of our country were virtually all physically constructed during the last years of the nineteenth century and the first years of the twentieth. Mostly fashioned in a Prix de Rome tradition of pantheonic grandeur, these stone temples, harking back to a Roman rather than a Greek tradition of purpose, were created as storehouses for display and for the promotion of civic pride as well as the stimulation of a kind of ostentatious philanthropy. The timing was right. The new wealth of America had created a rash of collectors, the greatest among whom became patrons of the arts even before the days of income tax. These monolithic mausoleums were built to attract essentially successful people. As America was a success, it could only be assumed that all its citizens wished to become successful. The art museum managed therefore to become a symbol of the community's rise to prominence and sophistication. Only the largest and most successful of these art galleries have managed over the years to weed out and arrange the welter of objects with which they have been showered. Fortunately the dangers of the bequest requiring *everything* of the donor's to be shown at all times, a feature of the turn of the century, have now been thoroughly exposed, and the concept discredited.

But often, in all this chronicle of changing tastes and sentimental preservation the museum trustees or those individuals classified as pillars of the community have been aided and abetted by a small professional caste of pundits and aesthetes, the curators of the time, described by Francis Taylor as "those flattering High Priests of culture whose appetites are often larger than their stomachs and who persist in saddling future generations with irresponsible commitments in the elusive hope of richer and more immediate rewards." These genii, in alliance with their aspiring architect colleagues of the time, all admirers of the Corinthian column, created the temple storehouses which often today stand so aloof and cool, seemingly unrelated to the present. As César Graña has recently put it: "the Greco-Roman style which signals the presence of a civic sanctuary; in this, as in the untouchability of the objects and the hushed decorum demanded of the visitors, there is much that is symbolically and behaviorly religious in nature . . . the work of art conceived as a sacred object . . . a storehouse for art *originals*," [15] whose contemplation is an inward, religious experience.

In this role, teaching or explaining such objects becomes a secular task, viewed by some curators as a descent from the sacred to the profane.

The art museums thus embarked on a course which tended to ally them with dominant forces in the community, the civic boosters and the wealthy who were philanthropically inclined. As a result, pursuing collections and funds, they had gradually alienated themselves from three important kinds of people. Among these were the historians of art who, as a vitally important source of scholarship and taste-making, tended to remain in self-perpetuating clusters in universities where they could teach, using plates from published books or color slides as illustrations in their classes rather than preferable museum objects. On the other hand there were the artists, who, unless they were copyists, tended to be rather "angry young men," hostile toward marble palaces, allied to the folk, and to a considerable extent uninterested in works of the past. Finally there were the people themselves who most needed stimulation and help, a sense of color and variety added to their lives. These were the poor people, products of a self-perpetuating disease found in our cities. Such people were neither objects of pride to our civic boosters nor particular objects of concern to our aggressive middle class who had responded to the urge to better themselves. If the art museum had become a symbol only to the community leaders and those conditioned to the concept of getting ahead, who realized that art was a subject of elitist veneration and that culture should be subscribed to and taken in doses like vitamin pills, then of course it had failed. If the wonders of a fantastic collection like that of the Metropolitan Museum in New York, which demonstrates many of the stages in the cultural evolution of Western and Oriental man, cannot somehow be brought to the humblest among us, the agonistic slum dwellers, then the purposes of the organizing committee of the Metropolitan Museum of 1870, quoted earlier in these pages, have not been served.

The Metropolitan is the greatest among these treasure houses, but there are more than a score across the country of nearly equal merit. If art objects are only to remain on pedestals and never to be interpreted to the people who need the support of cultural relevance the most, then the process of polarization will have become complete.

Fortunately many museums, particularly those concerned with science, early embarked on another course. The words "public education" had begun to be taken seriously. The first school museum was established in St. Louis about 1903. The museum consisted of a traveling section and a display section. The traveling section, in six large rooms, contained some ten thousand boxes and packages of all sizes and shapes strapped and labeled, ready for delivery to classrooms. Each week some five hundred groups of museum materials were distributed to some one hundred and twenty-five schools, according to the selections made by the teachers from the museum catalogue, listing two thousand individual groups. At the end of the week the material had to be returned to the museum.

Four large display rooms on the second floor included a receiving station for donations and purchased material, as well as sample groups showing the types of exhibit materials on history, climate and customs of peoples and natural history throughout the world.[16]

Thus the concept of an alliance between a city school system and a public museum was made patent. Museums began training docents, men and women who could interpret exhibits, on the one hand, and relate them on the other to a syllabus being taught in a grade-school curriculum. This was new, but a welcome outgrowth from the original concept of what a museum could do to counter the erosive influences of the city itself.

Curators, meanwhile, in the natural history museums became involved in an increasing evolution of educational exhibits. From the concept of dioramas it was only a step to the attempt to synthesize exhibits in such a way as to explain principles of biology or phenomena of nature. The original cabinet or "open storage" concept, where case after case would be filled with the museum's entire collection of minerals or mounted birds on wooden pedestals, birds in one hall, mammals in another, insects in a third, began gradually to be modified. At first it was selective. Half of the dusty bird specimens would be withdrawn from the wooden cases, to be demounted and placed in study collections in the research laboratory away from public exposure as well as the full sunlight from gallery windows. Then, often over the complaints of the curators themselves, exhibit departments or exhibit specialists began designing cases that told a story, using a variety of labels and perhaps blending several classes of objects, a mammal predator, for example, killing a bird, its prey; a fox with a ruffed grouse in its jaws. Photographs or other methods of reproduction began to be used to illustrate scenes or describe environments. Supplementary materials for the exhibits could be expertly prepared—dried grasses painted realistically or plastic molded leaves, colored to suit the season and attached to branches. The great era of taxidermy and the creation of related accessories had begun, stimulated by Rowland Ward in England and William Hornaday in the United States.

School classes could be brought into the museum and lectured about everything, from space, using meteorites or photographs of the stars, to the world of raw nature using polar bears and wolves, or the pastoral landscape of cows and domestic farm surroundings from which the children were separated in their

75

concrete jungles. For how many generations now of city children
has the never-never land of the pastoral landscape of the nineteenth century poets and the Currier and Ives prints been evoked
by visits to museums and farmyard zoos?

In Western Europe meanwhile, and eventually in the United
States, the achievements of technology had stimulated the creation of museums of applied science. The Great Exhibition in the
Crystal Palace in London in 1851 and the Paris Exhibition of
1889 had dramatized the tremendous popular hunger for science
and technological exhibits. The second applied-science museum
as such was that in South Kensington in London, opened in
1853 and using some of the materials of the Crystal Palace. An
earlier collection of scientific instruments in Paris had become
a museum by 1814, but served essentially as a research center.
The Moscow Polytechnical Museum, founded in 1872, and the
Deutsches Museum of Munich, organized in 1903, as well as the
Vienna Technical Industrial Museum of 1918, all antedated
similar efforts to create science-educational museums in the
United States. All of these attempted to portray the conquests of
science using working models as well as a historical array of
objects. When well planned, as these museums were, a whole
new array of exhibits for public instruction could be presented.
At every age level, from school child to adult, visitors could
demonstrate the wonders of an internal combustion engine or
the development of the principles of physics. It seems curious
that the United States, most inventive of all, failed until recently
to develop the applied-science museum concept. Most such
science exhibits in this country have been created for fairs, for
business conventions or other similar ephemeral uses. There has
been far less public support for science museums, and virtually
no governmental or business support on any continuing or permanent basis.

In contrast to the unequal progress of museums at the turn of

76

the century, libraries began to show a slow but steady progressive evolution. The same period that saw the ambitious development of art museums as objects of pride and cultural showcases saw a conscious development of private and public libraries. Benefactors like Andrew Carnegie symbolized the urge to spread library resources across the communities of the nation. Great private libraries collected by the turn of the century began to find their way by gift into the growing university libraries or the great city libraries or historical collections. The need for historical and bibliographic scholarship was apparent and recognized far more effectively than was the need for museum scholarship in the areas of the humanities.

The great exception to this appears to me to have been the field of classical archaeology, strongly supported at a few centers such as Chicago's Oriental Institute, the Boston Museum, Harvard, the Metropolitan in New York and the University Museum in Philadelphia. Aside from this field, there seems to have been little recognition of the constructive cultural-historical role which art museums could play. For some poorly defined reason, classical archaeology has always been firmly segregated in the United States from New World archaeology, which is pursued by anthropologists. Classical archaeology is conducted by linguists in the classical or Bible languages, papyrologists, epigraphers and the like, who are equated somehow with art historians, or other scholars of the humanities. Thus an art museum on one side of a public park in a large city might have a scholar working on early cultural man of the dynastic period of Egypt. This scholar might be the only member of the curatorial staff who could be described as a pure research scholar, or he might be part of a small department, perhaps the single department in the museum dedicated to research in the field and publication of research results.

On the other side of the park, in a natural history museum, a research-minded scholar among a rather large staff of scholars in the general field of natural history might be working on man of the early Maya period of Mexico. Curiously enough these two scholars might never meet, going, as they do, to separate professional meetings, publishing in separate journals, and, if posted to universities, continuing to teach and perform research in separate departments. Not only would two such scholars be using similar field techniques in excavation, but they would be concerned with the cultures of types of man at roughly similar stages of cultural evolution. To make the matter even less understandable, the New World archaeologist would have colleagues in his natural history museum working on the cultures of the East, Indonesia, southeast Asia, the Ainus of Japan or the Siberian tribes.

For support of his classical excavations sponsored by the Oriental Institute in the nineteen-twenties, Professor Breasted would turn to wealthy individuals interested in reconstructing the world of the Bible lands—individuals who would make winter excursions up the Nile on picturesque lateen-rigged yachts called dahabiahs, or ride donkeys in the Holy Land. Meanwhile Professor Kidder at Harvard during the same era would be appealing for expedition support for archaeological work in Middle America from foundations dedicated to the support of science and education like the Carnegie Corporation.

It had indeed become apparent by the beginning of the twentieth century that an unspoken schism existed in scholars' minds about the history of mankind. Art and culture were an obvious near-monopoly of the Western world and the highest civilizations from which our Western world derived—the Greeks, Egyptians, Jews and Babylonians. Of course, to the East one could not quite exclude the Indians, Chinese and Japanese. The artifacts of these peoples belonged in art museums, although they rested on a different plane of culture. Their civilizations had crossed some invisible threshold, and objects from these cultures were revered as true art, to be cherished in some cases as part of our own true antecedent culture and in other cases to be admired as being worthy of the accolade of true aesthetic appraisal.

Objects which represented the culture of the primitive races of man were the specialty of the anthropolgist, whose discipline, anthropology, rested on the uncomfortable assumption that the study of early man was somehow akin to biology. Anthropologists were not supposed to be interested in the Greeks or the Bible, but rather to concern themselves with Red Indians, noble savages, and, of course Stone Age man. Perhaps, although this was dangerous ground, they might even be concerned with missing links? Only in France, meanwhile, had a museum of man been created, the Musée de l'Homme, founded in 1877. Although called Museum of Man, it is sad that no decorative or folk art of Western man is included after Neolithic times. The arbitrary distinction is still maintained.

It has always seemed to me curiously undignified and rather unsophisticated as well that museum attitudes had become so polarized by the end of the nineteenth century and the beginning of the twentieth. The crux of the matter in America seems to have stemmed from Americans' attitudes about themselves and their origins. It is not only an artificial segregation, but it is philosophically untrue, and therefore spiritually degrading to assume that Western man of Mediterranean origin, with a few selected Orientals thrown in, has the hegemony of all that is aesthetically true and beautiful, to which we reserve the special accolades accorded the highest expressions of man. The result of this mumbo-jumbo of ours is expressed in the reverence and worship accorded to art in its chaste temples. On the other hand, research, somehow rather cold and unaesthetic, is the preserve of the natural history or science museum. A mythical chasm has been created in a twinkling between these two concepts, be-

79

tween what was once unwisely described as these two cultures.

The answer is of course that it is all one, that art and beauty and aesthetic appreciation may be found in the objects of nature as well as those of man at whatever stage of culture he is passing through. It is quite unnecessary to assume that a truly subjective aesthetic experience is reserved only for those enlightened mortals confronted, having been prepared by a proper cultural background, no doubt, for the first time with a Leonardo or a Praxiteles. It is also abundantly true that the early artifacts of the cultures of the Western world deserve far more scientific scrutiny than they have been receiving. Our museums should not be encouraged to compound the errors of their founding fathers—that great art deserves only worship and the refinements of the higher custodianship, and that science on the other hand is somehow separate, different and removed.* It has been

* In this connection it is somewhat encouraging to read a review by the well-known art critic John Canaday, in *The New York Times*, Sunday, June 30, 1968, of a new permanent diorama installation, "Man in Africa," at the American Museum of Natural History. Canaday says, speaking of the exhibit of African masks and fetish figures, that they are usually shown in this country as "pure works of art, following the point of view of most museums . . . divorced from specific anthropological reference. It is an art curator's point of view that I have generally agreed with, but 'Man in Africa' changed my mind. . . . Great works of art are exhibited alongside objects that, esthetically, are nothing more than attractive artifacts and others that are only functional objects of little esthetic distinction. But I found that this identification of works of art with the educational, ritualistic, governmental, scientific and economic functions that required their creation, tremendously enriched them." Bravo for Mr. Canaday! Although, as he says, we are mostly habituated to looking at art for art's sake, African sculpture suddenly looks better in this setting, in context.

gradually emerging that the task of the mid-twentieth century and succeeding years must be to attempt to dissolve the schism, to remove the gap between museums, and to recreate public understanding of the role of these paradoxical institutions.

CHAPTER FIVE

Museums of Today

The burden of my discourse so far has been to create a setting for the consideration of museums of today. What can museums do to emphasize to the public at large that they have a significant role to play in the community, and what can museums do to create a sense of unity of purpose among themselves? Parr, writing in 1950, expressed some of this concern in regard to natural history museums:

> Human influence [has] extended everywhere, and man's greatest and most direct concerns about nature were in regard to the effects of that influence both upon nature and upon man himself. But the natural history museums generally took very little account of these growing problems of civilization, and continued their overwhelming, and often exclusive, emphasis upon nature undisturbed by man, upon the rare and peculiar, upon that most vaunted possession of all—the extinct species, which can no longer affect human life one way or another—and upon the many interesting subjects deriving their significance from the theory of evolution, such as comparative anatomy, classification, biogeography and other.[17]
>
> That these subjects are technically essential for the progress of science and retain a high value for general education, we, as professionals, all know. And I wish to make it

perfectly clear that I am firmly convinced of the absolute need for continuing them in the programme of our museums. But I am equally convinced that they are far from constituting an adequate programme in the light of *modern* conditions, and far from fulfilling the *duties* which our opportunities give us to be of service to a troubled world. [Italics mine.]

It is only through our service to the world at large that we shall be able to earn the support we need for our continued existence and the further development of our functions. The world of science alone cannot provide it. And from a layman's point of view it is, perhaps, not unreasonable to feel that he has already paid a fairly generous bill for having had his unfortunate ancestry pointed out to him [by exhibits of physical anthropology] and to ask how the rare, peculiar, and undisturbed relates to his own hopes and aspirations in a very disturbed world. . . .

To re-establish our position we must find, and adopt, a new mission. . . . The side of nature which concerns society most of all is not undisturbed nature, but nature as the environment of man, and that is the field in which the educational efforts of the natural history museums could make their greatest contribution to human thought, welfare, and progress today.

To most curators of departments of natural history, Dr. Parr's words written in 1950 still have an alien ring. The average curator of a museum, like the average professor in a university, wishes to live in peace, content to conduct his own research, which tends to be in fields unconnected with the stresses and strains of the interplay between human society and the environment. It has really only been since World War II that it has gradually become respectable for a natural history curator to speak of conservation problems or to be directly involved in causes and issues of the moment like environmental pollution. In this I side with Dr. Parr. I recall well, in my own case, being warned as a very junior professor in an academic department that my unexpected interest in conservation (and therefore in worldly problems) might reflect eventually on my own hopes for promotion up the faculty ladder. To be allied, however indirectly, with *publicists*, traitors to the groves of academe, could become a hazard. Latterly, Rachel Carson, with her influence in academic circles, has become a noted exception of course. Well, so be it. It has always seemed to me that a museum has an obligation to hold itself in readiness to prove the validity of its collections. Natural history collections serve inevitably as data banks, figures marked upon the clock face of environmental time. Interpretation of the data provided by collections can produce evidence of environmental change. It is like studying tree rings or interpreting pollen deposits in cores from lake bottoms. Specimens provide the sources for a kind of biological iconology in which their study allows one to extract conclusions about the populations of animal or plant species, their occurrence, distribution and fate.

What can museums do to create a sense of unity among themselves? In a discussion of the present-day role of museums, as understood by the International Council of Museums, W. Aubrey Cartwright (unpublished) states an egalitarian point of view.

"Museums, [the Council] believes, no longer exist to serve the cultural or social needs of a small elite. Instead, they have a dynamic educational function to fulfill. In the world's more prosperous societies, they exist to help man make better use of his leisure time. In the developing countries, they bring him face to face with the benefits of technology, the lessons and example of history and the value of culture, his own or other people's. While catering to the needs of the profession, the International Council of Museums bears in mind both the museum-going public and that public that does not have or has yet to discover museums."

Museums, then, are the principal unrecognized arms of education. They are unrecognized because they are forms of open education, that is, the exhibits are there. They can be taken or left alone. No teacher will mark you or grade your paper as it were, for looking at them. Thus, museums have little direct relevance to schools or colleges who think of them as available public facilities, peripheral to the main issue, that do not have to be supported. Museums have no alumni associations and little if any organized constituency. How then can their work achieve recognition?

What do people say casually when they hear you work in a museum? "Oh, you work at the Smithsonian? How interesting. I went there once with my high school class. That's when I saw the *Spirit of St. Louis"; or, "Oh, I love the Smithsonian. We try to take the kids there on a Sunday." All of us who work in museums know these sorts of reactions. We all know the crowds as we press through on our way to a meeting or another laboratory. We know what we think about museums as places to work, but we are endlessly in the dark about what everyone else thinks.

Public educational programs are an obvious enhancement of the casual visit, the occasional need to return to view splendid and challenging things. And museums in this country are fulfilling this role at an expanding rate. More than 60 percent of our museums have guided tours of some sort, about 45 percent have lectures, and about 35 percent have temporary or changing exhibitions. All of this is of great value in public education. Twenty percent of our museums have children's programs, and these too, as adjuncts to school education, are vital.

But beyond this museums must establish themselves as essential educational institutions equal to or supplementary (but still essential) to all levels of educational activities from preschool to post-doctoral. They must make known that they supplement and enrich teaching at elementary and secondary levels in science, history and art. A conscious effort must be made to interrelate museum education programs with school and college programs of instruction. This effort is a considerable one for a variety of reasons. Education today is a highly organized phenomenon. More and more, departments of education at the city, state, and Federal level are organizing the accrediting of teachers, the teaching of teachers, and finally, the content of instruction. There is nothing wrong with setting standards for constantly improving the quality of education while trying to keep up with the boom, the crisis of quantity. But in this effort to give greater numbers of people some sort of "ticket of admission," some sort of diploma into a new, happy free world, a great society indeed, the values and the exposure that museums have to offer tend to get left out of the reckoning. There is an omission, a gap here, and it must be closed.

There are reasons for the existence of this gap. Museums themselves have been slow to attempt to close it. They have not tried to sell their wares to school supervisors. Individual museums have developed splendid areas of cooperation—the Virginia Museum of Fine Arts in Richmond, the Maryland Historical Society, the Peabody Museum at Yale. The Toledo Museum of Art has free art and music classes to which 2,500 children come every Saturday. Almost 400 classes from the schools come for a regular program of eight monthly museum visits each year, while about 1,000 adults attend regular college courses, and of these some 500 take the courses for university credit through the University of Toledo. Our National Gallery of Art in Washington provides films, film strips, and film lectures with recorded texts to schools and circulates traveling exhibits. The statistics are impressive. In one year traveling exhibits were booked 1,299 times; 2,446 slide lecture sets were circulated in 9,487 bookings. The total audience reached is estimated at over 2,000,000 persons in twelve months; and in the period 1960–1966 these materials had reached 3,074 cities in fifty states. Three of the recorded lectures are in French and are used by language teachers.

Overall, however, programs of this sort have not caught on. One of the reasons I have suggested elsewhere is our general high rate of literacy. We assume today that one can read about objects. They can be illustrated in books. It is not, therefore, necessary to touch them. In order to be an educated person, in order to be granted that diploma, one doesn't have to savor tactilely the texture of objects, to read them manually, to hear records of the sounds of the audible world. And yet, many people are not really born only to be literate. Many people are born with "illiterate" talents to read with their hands and ears, to develop a comprehensive talent for living only with the whole of the senses. Many highly creative and inventive people, as we all know, are much less interested in reading than departments of education would have us believe. Much pioneering work in the preparation of our citizens for adult life remains to be done in these threshold areas where education has somehow left off. Philanthropic foundations are always said to be interested in innovation. If this is true, they should help the world of museums to study problems of the nonreader who is oriented to objects.

In the areas of graduate and post-doctoral education, by far too little attention has been given to the role of museums. In the universities, university museums have had a difficult role to play, attempting to make administrators, deans, and university presidents understand the reasons for their existence. Pictures on the wall of the university art gallery can be understood even if relegated to a secondary level of importance—far less important than books. Art somehow is known to be respectable, certainly fashionable, and of course it is a way of attracting donors and art-minded trustees. But science—what do those old bones, those fossils convey? No, university administrators tend to have heard that electron microscopes are fashionable and money-attracting, not old bones.

And yet, as I once pointed out, in one university museum where I worked, 40 percent of all graduate degrees given in one department and 30 percent in another were solely due to the presence of a museum and museum collections at that university. Important areas of our Government responsibility in geology, vital areas of our teaching in anthropology were filled with people who had graduated through these museum-related departments, people who had used the objects, the collections, in a completely meaningful way which could never be assumed through or by books. The world of professionally organized learning must get the point. Graduate and post-doctoral work can center in museums. Museum-oriented programs must be not only tolerated but encouraged in the universities, and exchanges freely entered into at all levels. Here again, foundations should realize that museums as a whole have been languishing in starvation corner. While some of our greater museums, especially in the field of art, such as the wonderful Metropolitan Museum, have achieved a signal measure of support from private or foundation philanthropic aid, the vast field of museums across this nation has received an inconspicuous share of Government, foundation, or individual private aid—less than 10 percent of such financial help.

The study of education and communication by objects and exhibits should be of special interest in developing nations, where large populations are in the process of making lightning adjustments to technology and the world of science and modern-

day life. In certain areas in Africa, important strides in education and cultural development are being made through the institution of new museums and museum techniques. In India
there should be an instant recognition of the value of exhibits,
of the open-education techniques of museums, to education in
that country. In his book, *The Museums of India*, written in
1936, S. F. Markham pointed out that a nation with one sixth
of the world's population had only 105 museums. Then, in 1967,
a register of museums in India and Pakistan, its combined population still representing about one sixth of the world's total, listed
only 274 museums in the whole subcontinent. This is extraordinary. Museums could be the most important single educational
tool in India today. With a population problem and a language
problem combined, here is the perfect opportunity for the development of imaginative new techniques, using displays and objects, to communicate ideas and to teach.

Professor Levi-Strauss has recently pointed out that there is
a particular problem in the developing nations. This is the question of the preservation and recording of vanishing cultures. The
proper documentation of a human culture different from twentieth-century technocracy is as important as almost any human
endeavor. Such cultures have been uniquely adapted to the natural environment. Their study may reveal hidden truths of
human ecology. Yet the remnants of indigenous culture are vanishing like errant windblown dust devils over the prairie. An
urgent activity for museum anthropologists would be the stimulation and training of indigenous linguists and cultural anthropologists from among the very tribal peoples who are vanishing.
By creating a dignified aura of self-examination and self-re-
search it might be possible to raise more rapidly the self-esteem
and pride in individuality of these marvelous people before they
trample the last remnants of their own uniqueness to death,
rushing to be like everyone else.

In the United States alone, some eighty-eight Indian dialects or languages are still unknown to any but the remaining tribal people who speak them, and in most cases those who still do so are composed of less than ten individuals. So cultures vanish, each one fashioned by chance, adjusted by the keening winds of primitive life to an original identity, sharpened by the selective pressures of life at the limits of human tolerance. What a tragedy it is for man to have lost so many of the examples of human adaptability that were there to be studied. Man faces an uncertain future full of stresses beyond imagining. It would have been better if we could have documented more of man's compensatory emotional and psychological reactions to stress as demonstrated in so-called primitive cultures. There is a great task for museum anthropologists in the remainder of the twentieth century to marshal themselves in the cause of what has been called urgent anthropology, the sophisticated recording and documentation of vanishing cultures.

There is another realm in museums for anthropologists. This is in connection with folk life or folk culture. Social scientists have much in common with students of the problems of ethnography and urgent anthropology. All over the world non-Western cultures are coming under the influence of industrialization and urbanization. People adapted to peasant agrarian life are becoming constantly assimilated into cities. And yet even under modern urban conditions we know that dominant patterns of folk culture stay alive, creating small exile residual elements in ethnic subcommunities. No one has charted the course so far, but there is a need, and therefore a path will emerge. Some sort of alliance will have to be created between historians and collectors of folk life objects, ethnomusicologists, anthropologists and social scientists to study and eventually to understand the adaptive significance of these tribal and clan cultures and their persistence in the slums and under the pressures of urban life.

Surely there are lessons to be learned here of the greatest importance for the future of urban communities and indeed urban
design. I would hope that eventually a new kind of museum
could be created, a museum of man, to study the persistence of
older cultures, folk life and folkways in the face of the pressures
of increasing homogenization of life today.

In this connection art museums or art collections would have
an important role to play. Attempting to classify art styles
within measurable series (and therefore defying the academic
humanist who pretends to despise measurements as smacking of
the "scientific"), Professor George Kubler speaks to the history
of transcultural diffusion in the colonial situation:

"Occasionally, as in the sixteenth-century Spanish conquest
of Mexico and Peru, abrupt military action replaced these mo-
tions of commercial and missionary penetration. Conquest was
followed at once by massive European substitutions of useful and
symbolic behavior for native traditions. Only the useful items
new and necessary to Europeans survived the wholesale destruction of the native American civilization (potatoes, tomatoes,
chocolate, etc.)" [18]

Not only did few art forms survive in this atmosphere of sud-
den cultural death, but a new arrested class of art forms proceeded to take its place in the colonial society. Kubler defines,
in this sense, a colonial society as one "in which no major discoveries or inventions occur, where the principal initiative comes
from outside rather than from within the society, until it either
secedes from the parent-state or revolts." Of course many im-
poverished politically independent societies may remain for ex-
tended periods in a similar dilapidated condition because of
economic limitations or cultural impoverishment. Beauty in
form and creation may exist, but such beauty and charm, often
described as primitive, exist architecturally, as in certain towns
in Latin America such as Antigua in Guatemala or Taxco in

Mexico, because of an aptness for setting, because of a mellow, relaxed standard, lacking in invention, simplified, repeated over and over in an ancient way. Innovation is lacking, and we relish their repetition and their quaint flavor as we do peasant costumes in central Europe, which celebrate vanished court costumes.

Many art museums have important collections of so-called primitive art, or of colonial art, which deserve study in the context of the persistence of cultures and rates of duration as opposed to change. This is a kind of applied research in connection with art collections of which the general public must be totally unaware. Yet it is the development of relevance for which museums seek. How can museums play a significant role in the world today? How can they classify their holdings, how can they measure their true value? As Kubler points out, it can be done in a topological sense, where relationships rather than magnitudes are the measurements and create the parameters of research. In some ways the survival of ethnic subcommunities in urban cultures can be described as holdovers of tribal subcommunities in pockets in former colonial cultures.

In this sense works of art appear to me to be useful, perhaps a somewhat banal, or at least an overly exaggerated, statement. Kubler feels that:

"The main point is that works of art are not tools, although many tools may share qualities of fine design with works of art. We are in the presence of a work of art only when it has no preponderant instrumental use, and when its technical and rational foundations are not pre-eminent."

When the latter occurs, then the object is functional, therefore not an object of art. I cannot agree with this, in the sense that an object of art *can* contribute a message, and if so it immediately becomes susceptible to use as an object in the race against time in which each of us is involved, the race to understand the exis-

tence of consciousness. If a painting is a genuine expression and
conveys something, no matter who painted it, then it has many
subtle messages to convey about aesthetic significance. Self-
expressive autotelic activity is a basic phenomenon not only in
man but in many higher animals as well. No doubt, in time
behaviorists will deduce evidence that this is an evolutionary
phenomenon deriving from harmonics and symmetry in design
in response to the environment. Professor Hutchinson in a pene-
trating essay on art forms and nature[19] has expressed something
of this sense of unity among museums:

> Today we enter an art gallery expecting to be delighted
> by the beauty of certain works of man; we enter a natural
> history museum expecting to be instructed in the workings
> of nature. There are also museums in which archaeological
> or ethnographical material is displayed to illustrate some-
> thing about man that is akin to natural history, and indeed
> the same point of view is apparent in the grouping of works
> of art in any modern art gallery, where the pictures are
> placed by schools and periods, *i.e.*, geographically and
> chronologically, just like fossils in a paleontological collec-
> tion. What seems often to be lacking, at least explicitly on
> the part of the intelligent public, is the realization that a
> number of objects in the natural history museum are of
> extraordinary natural beauty and that they should be
> valued quite simply as such, as well as for their scientific
> connotations. The question however of the nature of the
> beauty of the natural world and its relation to human art
> deserves more consideration than it is customarily given,
> and deserves such consideration quite specifically in the
> context of the natural history museum.
> If we inquire why we make a distinction between the
> work of art and the object of natural beauty, which inquiry

93

is a partial rephrasing of our original question, I suppose that at the present time the essential difference would usually be described in terms of communication or expression. What is valued in the work of art is supposedly not the sort of intrinsic beauty that we find in nature, but some evidence of a message from, or expression of, the personality of another human being, the artist who made the work. This concept however leads us into very considerable difficulties. The late Bernard Berenson said at the end of his life, of which seventy-odd years had been largely spent in problems of attribution, that it did not matter who painted a picture as long as it was a real picture. This obvious truth, coming from him, carries nonobvious overtones. In the more limited modern vocabulary that we are using, it may be rephrased that it does not matter who painted a picture as long as the picture is a genuine expression.

Although I think there are good reasons for separating art galleries and natural history museums, they still, even after more than a century and a half of autonomous development, may have much in common.

How true this is and how much more true it may be in the future. How then are museums to face up to the problem of a role of significance, and how are they to create unity, to close ranks? Currently there has been a good deal of debate among museum directors. Critics tend to deplore the advent of multimedia exhibits, of the overpopularizing effect on museums of the new mass culture. This is reflected in immense crowds, in exhibits of current fashionable art, in jam-packed social events, "openings," done with all the fanfare of a premiere at Grauman's Chinese Theater in Hollywood.

Many artists continue to deplore having to go to any museums at all, reflecting the wave of hostility of the futurists of the turn of the century. Museums then were condemned as "cemeteries," although the comparison hardly seems apt any more. The only present resemblance to cemeteries that I have found is in the world of demonology or witches' fantasy. An opening of an "op" or "pop" or psychedelic light and sound show in a modern art gallery today bears a strong resemblance to a witches' Sabbath. I recall the painting by Gustave Doré illustrated in Paul Christian's *Histoire de la Magie* showing Lucifer presiding over a midsummer night's orgy in a cemetery complete with capering warlocks, male and female werewolves and related pixies both baleful and benign. But this is a superficial impression perhaps. What is true and what does confuse the critics as well as the die-hards who merely wish the museums to remain cozy cemeteries of the past is that we are in a state of profound transition. If museums are to weather this transition then they must experiment and probe until they have found a new series of responses to the selective pressures shaping our culture.

There is a sadness in the presence of television in all our homes today. For the most part, what it depicts mistily is so pedestrian. That pale corneal eye, Cyclopean, staring, gray, in every living room, bedroom or kitchen has, however, one overwhelming advantage. Its signal advantage is that it is possessed individually by the viewer, to be all one's own, raising no sense of antagonism or fear-hostility in the young as parents often do.

In October 1967, in a rather odd confrontation between museum professionals and Marshall McLuhan[20] on the subject of the communications inherent in the encounter between museums and the visiting public, Dr. McLuhan, who in the manner of oracles of old tends to speak in riddles, made one or two very telling comments. Referring to television he said, "Today, people over twenty-one can't adjust. We're all a lost generation. In our sensory lives we will never make the switchover. Only those coming up through the nursery will."

95

Although I don't agree that it is impossible to learn a new language after one reaches the age of twenty-one, it may be harder. In any case it is worth realizing that virtually half of our population today, and the younger half at that, speak a slightly different language from the other half. To create a sense of harmony between the dialects is vital. By using open, nondidactic techniques museums can go far toward helping to solve this new communications gap.

The brilliant young director of the International Council of Museums, Huges de Varine Bohan, rightly warns us of the future of museums. Either the museums will transform themselves into an activist role or, as he writes, "either the mutation will take place or the museum as a living institution will disappear. Petrified into a state of passive conservation, it will be nothing but a static cultural archive centre, oblivious of its responsibilities and remote, if not entirely removed, from those who most require it."

For us there is much to learn and not much time in which to do so.

CHAPTER SIX

Museums and the Future

What shape or form will museums of the future represent? What could happen to bring museums together into a common understanding of their present difficulty? How will it be possible to create a state of opinion among them which will welcome change and evolution? As Robert Hutchins recently said in a convocation speech at the University of Chicago (in 1967), "The most obvious fact of contemporary life is the rapidity of change. . . . Since there is no such thing as instant education, the search must be for the means of coping with problems, issues and phenomena now totally unforeseen," and he goes on to say that we cannot educate by training and by transmitting information. To do so is to guarantee only the development of skills for acquiring prosperity and power, not for the creation of understanding, and, incidentally, to add to the sense of confusion and frustration possessed by many undergraduates today.

The average person, then, who comes to work in a museum is a product of our present-day educational system, a system which tends to teach complacency along with skills, which tends to close off inquiry as it may be related to one's specialty, and which has taught, as Hutchins calls them "the tricks of the trade," at the same time that premature sclerosis has set in.

If this dilemma faces the museum professional by the very fact of his having been educated, it is going to be difficult to

97

maintain a spirit of inquiry in a museum setting. But fortunately museum professionals are lucky, at least at present, in that a career in museums is still not greatly popular. It is not thought of as one of the more stereotyped roads to success. In Hutchins' words, then, a museum today has much more chance of behaving like a university than do many universities, which by trying to do the popular, accepted thing of training for skills and information transmission, have long since become multiversities, signing away their birthright in the process. The university, in theory at least, is a community of scholars, some older than others, more involved in teaching. In such a community everyone is prepared for independent study. The ability to think for oneself is paramount, and furthermore, no one is involved unless he has the interest and capacity to join in the work.

To my way of thinking, such a definition of a university more aptly fits a museum nowadays. Sometimes my only concern is that I may talk too loudly or write too boldly and so let the secret out. This would perhaps be a mistake, for any such environment is a somewhat exclusive one, and if it were to become fashionable, the law of diminishing returns would set in. To me one of the advantages of working in a museum is that it is an unfashionable environment. This, then, gives museum research workers the opportunity to work and think unconventionally.

Although the publicly accepted stereotype of a museum is a place for the preservation and conservation of objects, and although this is a highly valuable objective in itself, I have tried to point out that this is only a part of the whole. Of course, the obligation to preserve and protect objects, using techniques ranging from conservation methods to schemes for cataloguing so that the information involved in the object can itself be retrieved, is central to a museum. However, the object is merely a visible symbol of an intellectual process; the act of storage is a tangible form of banking information. The information may be presented to the viewer by sight, contact via touch, sound perception, or other sensory means including smell or taste. Professor McLuhan feels that of the senses sight is the only civilized sense we possess because it provides detachment, while all the others create a sense of involvement. I do not agree with him. I think hearing does not necessarily create involvement, especially in present-day life, when the decibel rate of ambient noise is high and buffers us. The visitor to a museum with a transistor radio clamped to his ear is not involved in the sounds. The noise is merely part of his personal cocoon of withdrawal, of non-involvement. So all senses can really be taken or left; even the most intimate become numb from overuse, or can be "turned off," as it were, by an exercise of will.

My central conviction that a museum is indeed a university stems from the persuasion that objects which are maintained and preserved in such a setting are there for a reason. They are there to communicate to us, those of us who have bothered to preserve them at all. This is an age of communication. As it is then we must indeed experiment on how to bring these objects into communication with ourselves. The process involves all levels of research. Among research specialists in the history of art it is commonly accepted that perceptiveness based on experience and background knowledge is critical in the formation of judgments. Dr. Herbert Friedmann in an interesting essay,[21] points out the close resemblance between the process of coming to a conclusion by an historian of art and this same process by a natural scientist—a comparison which should, I hope, both please and surprise the humanist. The art historian and the biologist go through similar processes of inductive reasoning based on training and experience. Friedmann shows that in the process of discovery and classification "a zoologist confronted with an unnamed and undocumented specimen, and an art historian called upon to identify a painting of unknown origin, provenance and

99

authorship . . . both [in the process are] being guided, almost without having to think about it, by [their] general knowledge and past experience . . . involving a vast and scattered literature, as well as the direct examination of specimens and the comparison with related ones."

He goes on to compare the intellectual process of the creations of synthetic imagination in the biologist and the art historian. In the case of a hypothetical missing link in the world of marine invertebrate classification, the discovery of *Neopilina*, an ancestral mollusk, vindicated the characterization of its "hypothetical ideation" by a biologist, Dr. Knight. In the case of Bernard Berenson's group of paintings of a mystery artist who fell between the works of other well-known painters and related in style to the Florentine master Ghirlandajo, time eventually proved him right. The work belonged to a single, previously unknown painter, Bartolommeo di Giovanni, its identification based on small, trifling characters of style, most of them of the least importance in the overall visual result.

These sorts of learning and skills must essentially be acquired in museums. The similarity of the intellectual processes involved is a reaffirmation of the similarities of museum research, whether performed in an art gallery or a natural history museum. The development of criteria, the sharpening of perceptive, yet subjective, modes of judgment, is often construed as unscientific by experimental scientists. It is merely that the process is different from theirs. Darwin put two and two together in an intuitive sense by field observation and reading, but without experimental proof. The end result was science even though experimental scientists remain dubious. Lasswell [22] has described the fact that many specialists are apprehensive of their capacity to withstand the temptation to make biased or dishonest observations, to suppress unfavorable findings, or to neglect or distort theoretical points. It is comforting to specialists in art history and natural history to find that the identity of their methods of appraisal is not a mere coincidence, but that the methods have reality and serve to corroborate the soundness of the techniques, each for the other.

If, then, the museum presents a special arena for research, one of the most cogent subjects for inquiry could be one that should concern social scientists and educators alike. That is the study of the awakening of interest. At the root of most of our troubles as human beings is the lack of any sort of interest at all except for self-preservation. Of what use are any of the proposed panaceas for the preservation of evolved civilization or the maintenance of cultures, if the majority of living people simply don't care? If the education industry does not create people who are interested in the world about them during their one single life, then education is, above all, a failure.

I would contend that museums are the greatest available laboratory for studying the problem of how to create interest, and that this problem is central to our quest for survival as people. Surely by now we should all realize that the perfection of mechanical techniques for living is not enough. What avails it to be surrounded as a race with all the wonders of technological wizardry, temporarily secure on our plundered planet, and simply not care?

Could it not also be added that by making people interested, aware therefore of the sum of their surroundings, we are doing something more? The creation of cultural interests may be a step on the eventual road to salvation. Culture begets aesthetics. Aesthetics involves preservation, and more, conservation. The scientists of the Plymouth Marine Laboratories, summing up the "Torrey Canyon" disaster,[23] say pungently: "We are progressively making a slum of nature and may eventually find that we are enjoying the benefit of science and industry under conditions which no civilized society should tolerate." If the voters of the nations tend to lack interests, they can obviously only dimly perceive where their cars, refrigerators and television sets are taking them.

The great advantage of the museum, then, as a possible study laboratory for interest arousal is that the public visitor doesn't know he is being tested. Watch him enter—any one of the two hundred million people who annually enter a museum in the United States. Why has he come in? How can we find out? The museum is likely to be a large, strange building. Going into it therefore can be a different experience, reserved for some separate, some special time, almost an event. The process, except perhaps for coming in out of the rain, or looking for a handy washroom, is likely to involve curiosity, already an involvement. Having any curiosity at all already means something just a bit positive, favorable to the individual. This whole act is hard: it may involve putting on different clothes, being in different surroundings, getting onto a bus or into a car. Unfortunately for many people, especially poor or poorly educated people, or certainly incurious people who already have no or very few interests, this act involves crossing a threshold outside of ordinary life. The strain may be such that the most deprived will never come, and never be observed or tested.

But the sociologist must start somewhere in order to watch and try to test the museum visitors who do come. They are the best available raw material. It appears likely that the development of voluntary testing equipment for a museum lobby or gallery space is now possible. Some of this work has already been done recently in this country at the Milwaukee Public Museum by de Borhegyi, who has attempted through various exhibits to test public reactions.[24] Suppose we could go further and set up four or five consoles so that four or five people could step up casually on their own and manipulate the buttons of each console, independently, to solve a problem in aesthetics or science, or to project the solution of a choice of some problem for the future. Using television screens, the museum visitor could select one of several options, watch the problem unfold on the screen in front of him, and volunteer his own suggested answer. In the Czech Pavilion at Expo 67 in Montreal there was a combination movie-narrator performance called Kino-automat, in which the audience was presented with a simple choice by the narrator as the film progressed. Should the policeman's frantic signals be heeded or not as the car went rocketing past him on a crowded street? Two buttons on each chair arm gave everyone a chance to vote while the film was temporarily arrested. The majority vote was flashed on the screen, and in theory the driver of the runaway car stopped, or else went dashing on in pursuit of the other car. I suspect that the audience vote was always the same in this case, but in any case the audience received the impression of a choice having been made, and obviously was intrigued and dazzled by the novelty of the game.

In our proposed museum tests it should be possible to have several thousand persons a day make such individual choices by operating their own console buttons, then to have the information recorded and banked on tape. Novel programs of this sort could be arranged by social psychologists so as to acquire millions of responses voluntarily and without even the pressure of having to open a piece of fourth-class mail, or answer a telephoned pollster's questions. The contact would be far more random and involuntary.

Something along the way in such a study might give us a clue to why people in a museum liked round objects or square objects, stuffed elephants or steam engines, paneled rooms or Eskimo igloos complete with Eskimo manikins. We might find out not only why people react to things in a certain way, but what these reactions stem from, and if interest has been created or is capable of being created by the very reaction itself. We would of course like to go further, find out who these people are, what schooling they have had, and so forth—but I am becoming greedy. It would be necessary to experiment all along the line so as to avoid tiring the player of the game or making him self-conscious.

Some psychologists will complain that our samples of people to be tested would be biased, that we have only the typical middle-class visitor to choose from, but I would dispute this claim. In the first place, we have had this past year over fourteen million "visits" to the Smithsonian buildings, whatever that figure means. Certainly not every one of the millions of visitors, and not even every visitor that might have played our games had we had the machines in operation, could be described as a sociologist's stereotype of a typical American middle-class citizen. And besides, we could, if we had them, set up such gaming and testing machines in one of our neighborhood museums.

One of the shapes and forms that will be discerned for museums of the future must certainly be a neighborhood museum, for at least in its initial development it seems to me that this is an experiment for which the Smithsonian Institution should take some measure of credit and pride. The concept of bringing a museum out of its stated setting, its museum building, is not new. A traveling exhibition is a projection of the museum itself. The school visit by a museum docent with sample exhibits is another. Museums have even pioneered the bookmobile or traveling-library principle. The Virginia Museum of Fine Arts has had a highly successful traveling program consisting of exhibits in trailer trucks traveling to rural areas or smaller towns in the State. The Bridgeport Museum of Science and Industry fitted up a trailer with a splendid exhibit on space which could be driven to one school parking lot after another and then used for a week or more by that school's science teacher.

But all of these programs overlooked rundown urban areas, areas of disadvantage and significant lack of opportunity. When

I was small these areas were always called slums, and their rows of poor, rundown houses, tenements. Now there are other sloganlike names for them such as "ghetto," which are trite from overuse and perhaps misapplied as well. Some of these rundown parts of cities are relatively pleasant quiet backwaters, some are merely gently dilapidated, while others, of course, are violent and, to us, jungly. The urban problem is upon us and beats on our ears or flashes out of the newsprint, or snarls at us from shattered shopfronts every day.

To a large extent, people from rundown neighborhoods tend to stay there. They tend not to be mobile, or to move much out of their district, except in a transient sense from slum to slum. Such people, referred to again by slogan phrases like "disadvantaged," are likely never to go into any museum at all. Here I agree wholeheartedly with the sociologists. Indeed such people may feel awkward going out of their district, badly dressed or ill at ease. They may easily feel lost as they wend their way along an unfamiliar sidewalk toward a vast monumental marble palace. They may even feel hostile. In Washington, D. C., a city where 262,000 people, or about one third of the total population (of the District), live just above subsistence level, it is hardly to be expected that large numbers of the poor can afford the bus fare for a trip to a museum, or the clothes either. In connection with a recent PTA program in Washington to sponsor trips for children and their parents to local attractions, a number of parents in one low-income neighborhood objected to the program. The parents, it was learned, felt that they did not have the proper clothing for such a venture; they preferred not taking part to the possible humiliation of conceivably being denied admission to places they might want to visit. If the above is true, then the only solution is to bring the museum to them. For of all our people, these are the ones who most deserve to have the fun of seeing, of being in a museum. Although private collectors may wish to keep their collections private, the responsible person in charge of a museum, no matter how recondite, esoteric or aesthetically rarefied his collection, must occasionally have at least a twinge of educational esprit, the merest modicum of egalitarianism or desire to improve the lot of his fellow man.

However, it is obvious in the case of a museum in a rundown neighborhood that the bookmobile concept won't do. Involvement is what is wanted, and a bookmobile museum in a slum implies something for nothing from rich folks somewhere else, a kind of charity, a handout, largesse in white gloves. Involvement can only be created if it is *their* museum. It must be on the spot, participated in by the people who live there. This was our principle in 1966 when we in the Smithsonian started looking about for a neighborhood which might want a neighborhood museum. We looked for a site, perhaps an abandoned movie theater or a grocery store, given up because some new chain store had taken over the district. Our one guideline was that the area must have stability, not be too full of transients or migratory unemployed. Preferably we wanted a block that contained a laundromat, that symbol of daytime neighborhood involvement, rather than too many bars.

We found the district in Anacostia, one of the areas of Washington which has changed a good deal since the days of the distinguished Frederick Douglass. Consultations with the Southeast Neighborhood House in Anacostia revealed an instant enthusiasm on the part of the local residents. With their help we decided to try, and we set out to rent an unoccupied theater which by chance was on the same street as a local school, and in the same block as a laundromat.

The auguries seemed good. A community advisory council was formed early in 1967, chaired by Mr. Alton Jones, Chairman of the Greater Anacostia Peoples, Inc., Mr. Stanley Anderson, later to become one of the first members of the new City

Council of Washington, Mrs. Marion Hope, Mr. Ben Davis, and a good number of willing volunteers, including a sergeant of the 11th Police Precinct, Andrew Salvas. My colleague, Charles Blitzer, was active from the beginning, and we depended heavily on the advice of Mrs. Caryl Marsh, who had worked with neighborhood social problems in Washington. Our Smithsonian Exhibits department, led by John Anglim and Ben Lawless, was keen to rush in from the start to remodel the small 400-seat movie theater, and Robert Shelton was assigned by them to draw up a design. Long and prayerful meetings (most of them in a local church) with the advisory council ensued before they decided on the framework of the exhibits, their focus and the degree to which a variety of exhibits might appeal to local residents. By June 1967 we had selected a director, Mr. John Kinard, a thirty-year-old Washington-born youth worker who had worked in the Neighborhood Youth Corps and the Office of Economic Opportunity. Under Kinard, who is vigorous and decisive, the exhibit plans were finally completed and the work was begun. The seats were removed and a flat floor was installed with two single steps at intervals to take care of the slope. Six modules were constructed along the sides of the seating area, two to a section of the floor, so that each single step marked the partition between the modules. The exhibits resulted from a vast number of suggestions, primarily from the advisory council, but also from the Smithsonian staff curators. A complete general store, just as existed in Anacostia in the 1890s, occupies one corner. In it is a post office (which we hope to get a license to operate), old metal toys, a butter churn, an ice-cream maker, a coffee grinder and a water pump, all of which can work, and any number of objects of the period from kerosene lamps and flat-irons to posters and advertisements. There is another do-it-your-self area for plastic art, with, at present, volunteer class instruction. There are skeletons of various kinds, some of which can be put together, some disassembled. There is space for temporary art shows. There is a TV monitor system on the stage. Occupying one of the modules is a live zoo with green monkeys, a parrot and a miscellany of animals on loan from the National Zoological Park. A great success was a shoebox museum in an A-frame structure, full of wooden shoeboxes containing bird skins (in celluloid tubes), mammal skins, shells, fossil specimens, pictures and slide projectors for intensive handling and study. A behind-the-scenes museum exhibit of leaf-making, silk-screen techniques, casting and modeling, gives an additional outlet for instruction. All of this, to the tune of crashing hammers, scraping saws and slapping paintbrushes, took form in two and a half months.

The grand opening, attended by an 84-piece band, two combos, and a block party with speeches and klieg lights, took place on September 15, 1967. A local group of Trail Blazers had painted the nearby fence separating the museum from the next property with a stylish "primitive" mural of life in Africa. The desolate surrounding lots were spruced up, and one of them decorated temporarily with Uncle Beazley the dinosaur, hero of the story *The Enormous Egg*. One of the striking byproducts of the opening was the improvement in the appearance of the block. Several storefronts and houses were newly painted. The local utility company branch, with friendly and unexpected solicitude was hastily painted and landscaped with shrubbery, greatly enhancing its previously dreary-looking brick premises. The whole place began to look almost as smart as the swagged bunting draped on the old theater marquee, now rechristened as the Anacostia Neighborhood Museum.

The financing for all of this had to be raised from private sources, for the Federal government is, presumably quite rightly, only rarely interested in innovations of a sociological nature.

This was an experimental project; for a museum, especially for the sedate Smithsonian, it could be described as "offbeat." We estimated that the first year we would need to raise between $60,000 and $75,000, and by the fall of 1967 we had about $75,000 in hand, mostly from three foundations—the Carnegie Corporation, the Anne S. Richardson Fund and the Meyer Foundation. When in early 1968 we realized that all this would cost more, we received a challenge grant from the Irwin S. Miller Foundation, and small private contributions from interested citizens have been slowly but steadily coming in. At this juncture my colleagues and I estimate that a neighborhood museum can run on something under $125,000 a year, once it is under way, with a flexible staff of four full-time employees as well as volunteers, and contract or volunteer work from exhibits specialists. Changing exhibits are of the first importance, for any new experience such as a new museum can of course pall in time.

The results so far in mid-1969 are hard to assess. Anacostia has a known population of nearly 200,000 persons, 41 percent under eighteen, 78 percent nonwhite. The median family income, compiled from census records, is $3,430. In the first twenty-one months some 102,049 visits had been clocked in to the museum, a building about 100 feet long and 60 feet wide, with a tiny mezzanine floor for offices in the former projection-booth area. Obviously something is happening. School classes are being taught there. A local businessman has donated a school bus to drive children to the main Smithsonian buildings for our own Saturday-morning classes. These are, of course, children who would never otherwise enter the main marble mausoleums on the Mall.

There are no guards at the Anacostia Museum, and there has been no vandalism. Not a feather or a fossil has been stolen. What is the mystery of this equation: No guards = no losses and no vandalism? The only valid answer of course is "because it is their museum, not ours, and they can be proud of it."

Curiously enough, many people who at the very least belong to the Book-of-the-Month Club find all this singularly uninteresting. "You have no business fooling around with all this stuff," one man told me. "I'd as soon burn them as lend you any of my masterpieces."

I was tongue-tied, as most people are when harangued suddenly, or perhaps the word hectored is a better one. But I did try to tell him one thing which pleased me about our experiment. I wanted to keep the Neighborhood Museum rather individual, just itself, different from the rest of the Smithsonian. It is *their* Museum in a real sense, not ours. However, after a while I had wanted to have a small discreet sign put up, saying in effect, "If you want more of this, take the such-and-such bus line over to central Washington and go to Constitution Avenue Northwest between Fifth and Fourteenth Streets and you can see more of it, on the Mall." I didn't know quite how to put it unobtrusively, but the idea haunted me. How to get people who never went anywhere to go to a museum where somehow change and evolution in their own lives might be set in train? Surely, if museums of the future are to be valid, they must be of use, must communicate to the very people who need them most.

One day I took Harold Howe II, then United States Commissioner of Education, to see the Anacostia Museum and then to have a sandwich in the little noisy restaurant next door. We entered the vestibule of the old theater, past the ticket booth, now gaily decorated with posters and exhibition news. Inside John Kinard was standing with a group of several men to whom we were introduced. Suddenly one of them, a giant of a man in a rough jacket, turned to me and said:

"You know, Mr. Ripley, I've lived my whole life right here. I drive a truck, see, and I go everywhere. I been up and down that old Constitution Avenue all my life. I've never been in those big [accented] buildings. I'd be scared to. But now—you know, I'm going into that old Smithsonian of yours. Yes sir, you're getting me cultured before I know it."

And so I heard what I had come to hear.

CHAPTER SEVEN

Museums and the Future 2:
How Many Table Leaves?

There are many problems associated with museum exhibits for which as yet there seem to be neither answers nor even a degree of consensus. Museum exhibits are like a buffet table spread out for the delectation of the wedding guests. At the last moment the anxious housewife, knowing that a good number of guests are coming from far away and may need added sustenance, or perhaps a hot casserole dish if the weather has turned cold, says that she will just have to put another leaf in the table. And so the groaning board gets another leaf and an addition to the generous and tempting clutter. Turkey is piled upon ham, and a salmon mousse on a hot cheese dish and a welter of hospitality is the result.

No one has ever been able to decide what the public wishes to see in a museum. No one knows who the public really consists of and so no one knows whom to question, let alone what to ask. Historical museums often start off as intensely personal private collections of one individual. Often a small town's historical society supports a historic house or similar museum formed originally by a single collector. If the town fathers or the society continue to maintain it, usually with severely limited funds, the person in charge, be he called curator or director— often an honorary position, or perhaps one with a janitor's salary—is expected to maintain essentially the status quo. The original printed labels are jealously guarded, fruit of the certainty of the original collector. They are often grossly misleading as to provenance of the objects, either because of ignorance or sloth of those in charge, or through fear of offending the donor's heirs, or perhaps just to save money, as changing labels is expensive. This mournful cemetery of historical objects of uncertain identity arouses a mental image that causes trained historians to stay away and tends to create a permanent block in the attitudes of historical scholars toward museums.

Labels are at the heart of the museum dilemma. Assuming that they can be changed, and that the museum has a budget for this and the staff to make the initial effort for accuracy, there is then the question of what to put on them, if indeed there are to be labels at all. To begin with, a room or a hall is open to the public. There are cases of some sort containing objects. There may be, indeed there usually are, too many objects. The board is groaning with hospitality and more leaves are being added to the table all the time.

But no one knows the wedding guests. We cannot do more than hazard a guess who they are. Are they tourists, townspeople, adults, children? Do they have a high interest quotient or a low interest quotient? Do they have any interest at all? Is anyone coming at all? No wonder the writer of labels is oppressed at the thought of what to say.

One anthropologist colleague of mine feels that the museum collections should be severely culled for objects of both beauty and the symbolic exposition of the culture they represent, and that they should just be set out in the cases and left there, without labels, presumably for the visitor to make up his own mind, or perhaps to have a subjective aesthetic (or spiritual) communication.

The opposite pole consists of the curator who insists on intellectual domination, the relentless pedagogue who must explain every detail. A single object in a case must be smothered in words, written words, sometimes spoken words if he can get his hands on one of those hearing-aid lecture tours which can be rented from the attendant at the door. Such a curator is merely frustrated that he cannot seat every helpless visitor in a chair and lecture him to the brink of collapse on every arrowhead, for example, and every modification of that arrowhead to show varieties of stone used, variant shapes and degrees of skill in chipping or flaking.

It is obvious that labels are better than no labels. It is also obvious that there is an elusive moment for education here. Some grain of mustard seed may be dropped into fertile soil to sprout another day, sending a youth who is *interested* in something off to a library or to college. But the labels are inherently dangerous. Label fatigue must be avoided, too.

Another colleague has a good suggestion, I think. In a museum exhibition case, let the objects tell a story, and let the labels help to tell it, but in four degrees. Let the top label of the case say, for example, "Easter Island Artifacts" in 324-point capitals. Below this there might be an attractive design made up of Easter Island objects pleasingly lighted, and hung or placed on inconspicuous brackets. Beside each object there might be a severely simple label in 30-point type, saying "wooden figure of the Moai Kavakava style," or "adze head," or whatever the object is.

For the third level, there might be a printed label off at the side of the case in readable type of 24-point size, perhaps silk-screened against a background of an Island scene taken from an illustrated travel book of the last century. This label, in two paragraphs, say, might tell something of the mystery of Easter Island and its people.

Finally the fourth level, in very small type, let us say in 14-point, might be at the bottom and side of the case, easily overlooked by most people, like a footnote, and might be a brief directory to titles of three of the best books on Easter Island. This last stage would be for the eager twelve-year-old, equipped with keen eyesight or his own magnifying glass, who really wanted to know all about Easter Island.

The symbolism is plain. Sixty percent of the visitors who happened to look at the case at all would be satisfied seeing the name "Easter Island." It wouldn't matter whether they recognized the name, had read Thor Heyerdahl's best sellers or not, or thought this name referred to the new island setting for the next Elizabeth Taylor-Richard Burton boom or bust. Thirty percent of the visitors would stop and actually read the names identifying the artifacts—a pretty high proportion. Seven percent would actually read the paragraphs about Easter Island. Thus three percent would be left to squat down, read the fine print and take notes.

This would take care of everybody except the out-of-town student who would write in to the curator or the director of such and such a museum to say that he was writing a term paper on Easter Island and would someone please send him all the available information on this place for his paper, return postage not included. This is a continuing trial that all museums live with— whether they are capable of answering or eager to answer or not is no matter. The Smithsonian alone answers over thirteen thousand of these queries each year, mostly on dinosaurs and American Indians, but also on how to tell a genuine Stradivarius violin—the latter so common a question that the Institution has prepared a printed reply. But the mail really has little or nothing to do with the museum visitor. It comes or goes throughout the year like gentle rain, irrespective of the number of visitors.

In general, it can be taken for granted that labels are better than nothing, although I am assuming that any such labels are well written. This assumption is not always true. The ability of a curator to write does not in itself mean that he can write a

115

label. In general, label writing looks deceptively easy, but the text usually needs to be edited and refined after it has been drafted by the person who supplies the facts.

One of the problems for the label writer is that adults, unless they are bringing children as a duty several times running, simply develop fatigue rather rapidly and tend to overlook all labels. Adults who come into a museum, as Mr. Hume[25] has pointed out, tend not to come again or to lose interest rapidly, especially if they are part of a tour group, unless there is a sympathetic guide or docent to kindle their attention. Various experiments have been designed to supplement labels, from the rented audioguide system to pushing a button in front of the exhibit in order to hear a brief lecture recitation, all the way to the docent on tap by appointment. The Musée de l'Homme in Paris even tried having graduate students stationed at certain hours in parts of the museum. If the student noted a group showing interest in front of a particular case of South Sea Island artifacts, for example, he or she would wander over, inquire if they would like to hear about the contents of the case, and if the answer was in the affirmative, launch into a few brief explanatory comments. This is an ideal and potentially effective procedure which we are trying at the Smithsonian in the Fine Arts Gallery at present, using volunteer guide-guards, who wear a blazer instead of a uniform, and are there to provide answers to questions.

Nowadays the problem of language is becoming something to reckon with. As museums become established in areas with tribal or other plural cultures and languages, where labels are meaningless because of language barriers or illiteracy, there is the question of which language or dialect to use and how many varieties to budget for. In the Papua-New Guinea Museum, in view of the many tribal dialects of the visitors, the labels are in English and the docent is prepared to lecture in English, Motu or Pidgin. He simply cannot master all the tribal dialects. In Zambia it has been noticed that docents using local languages tend to raise tribal jealousies. In Sarawak, English is used for labels, as this is still the administrative language, but the Dayaks have a variety of different languages, from the coastal peoples to the mountain dwellers, and would probably prefer Malayan as a lingua franca. Even in American cities today, foreign tour groups or ethnic subculture groups would probably be delighted and highly interested if leaflets at least explaining museum halls could be prepared in four or five of the most common languages. In Romania, at the archaeological sites along the Black Sea coast, the labels are automatically in Romanian, French, Russian, German and English, a vital concession to the tourist.

Another of the exhibit problems today is that of how much or how little to show. It continually arises as an argument between curator and exhibits staff. The outcome is a space problem which continually bedevils museum directors. The tradition of gradually withdrawing objects from public view commenced in the nineteenth century. Critics like John Ruskin and museum directors like Charles Eastlake of the London National Gallery, and Louis Agassiz, the Harvard biologist, had proposed what was called the bipartite concept: exhibit materials on show, and study collections for the connoisseur and specialist. These selective innovations were started in galleries of paintings and in arrays of scientific specimens. In the first instance the old tradition of wall-to-ceiling displays of paintings locked frame to frame like wallpaper gradually gave way to the single-line concept, where a work of art can be admired for itself, and each one glanced at or studied alone. The implication here is that the public is better served when it can see and appreciate pictures one at a time. The old idea of pictures being on show for the informed, the amateur, largely disappears in the process. The iconographic significance of a period or an artist's circle, the

117

harmonious interrelationships of a group of painters in time as a whole, can no longer be afforded with the single-line concept. Theoretically this solution of fewer paintings, each standing out in its own space, is more aesthetically pleasing, but it is less educational. In the process something is lost, but the art gallery has its own excuses for that. Whereas the nineteenth-century approach of comparative study brought back connoisseurs time after time with notebooks and journals to fill, the present assumption of art galleries is that they have a mass market to contend with, that the public can be presented with a few carefully chosen masterpieces before which individuals can perform their own reveries and private worship, but which cannot be thought of as more than scratching the surface of a period or a style, a circle of artists or a school. The minor masterpieces are stored or exchanged or out on loan in the process—sometimes even sold off.

Perhaps this is another reason why historians of art tend to be unhappy with art-gallery directors. The objectives of the two types of people run parallel only at times. There is no single purpose uniting them. Convinced that the public is blasé to everything except known stated masterpieces, convinced that crowds and numbers matter, the art-gallery director restricts his permanent galleries as much as possible to surefire hits, and reserves his temporary galleries to traveling or temporary shows, which may occasionally concentrate on bringing together the more historically worthwhile concept formerly seen in the old crowded days of frame-to-frame exhibits, the *whole* of an artist's or a school's or a circle's work.

The science museum reached the single-line concept for a slightly different reason—not only to alleviate the crowded look of the cases, the groaning board. The value of many of the individual specimens quickly became apparent, and so material was taken off show to the back storage or study areas where research students could handle or work with it. The result was to achieve the same aesthetic improvement as the art museum but at the sacrifice of the detailed comparison and inspection by the intelligent amateur of a sample of every class or type of creature in the animal, vegetable or mineral world. A few museums, conscious of public interest, keep a room or a section available for a synoptic sequence of every bird or mammal or reptile found in the area of the museum's location, so that the amateur can identify what he has just seen or collected on a field trip.

Something of the same sort of problem exists in the decorative arts. Collections of porcelain, glass, textiles or silver tend to arouse the curator to slip yet more leaves into the overladen table. How much should be shown? When the late James Rorimer came down from the Metropolitan Museum in New York to see the new hall designed for showing the Smithsonian's porcelain collections and, most notably, the newly presented Hans Syz collection, he was visibly thrilled as I walked him around the display. The magnificent cases, not too cluttered with objects, still allowed the visitor to compare periods, styles of treatment of design and, for once, compared the original Japanese and Chinese model pieces with the German, English and French resultant styles and design copies. A concession to the scholar was the creation of a separate side room in which a crowded array of all the different types were shown cheek by jowl, just like the synoptic suite of birds or mammals reserved for the hobbyists. Thus public exhibition was served by a rough adherence to the single-line concept, and extra side space reserved for the interested amateur.

"Now I realize that at the Metropolitan we simply have museum storage," Rorimer said, smiling at me wistfully as we parted.

Museum exhibits continue to provoke arguments between curators and exhibits specialists. The boom in public attendance

119

is a heavy drain on exhibits staff. More and more existing museums cut down on public exhibition space as storage problems increase and all the attendant amenities are thrust upon them. More staff is always needed: craftsmen, restorers, conservationists, carpenters, upholsterers. Space is at a premium for shipping and receiving, including temporary accessioning, inspection, minor repairs, carding, perhaps photographing. All of this work should be done preferably in a production line, near the loading-receiving dock so as to make for efficiency. Elaborate climate-control machinery often must be installed in existing facilities, making vast demands on space in cellars or attics. Ancillary lighting problems make old skylights difficult problems to wrestle with. The resulting aesthetics are often atrocious, but daylight illumination is now shown to be a danger even to oil paintings.

Then there are the services to be added, conference rooms, more offices, cafeteria facilities and rest rooms for staff as well as the public, public-relations areas, perhaps a built-in radio or TV studio, auditorium, sometimes a theater. It is no wonder that many museums today find that two-thirds of a building's space is so occupied, and the collections reduced to one-third. The resulting storage problem becomes then a fierce fight between those concerned with the aesthetics of exhibition, those who want to show everything, and those who want to make museum storage into a reality.

The curator's role in all this is one that requires a sort of superman. As Eisler[26] points out, today's art curator must be capable of being a courtier with the trustees upon whose constant approval his job depends, but he must also be a showman, an interior decorator, an administrator and a financier. American art museums still retain some of the attributes of a cultural club. The president and trustees are likely to be dilettantes of the arts to a degree, and beyond the qualities enumerated above, most trustees want: "curators who are primarily in the field of post-Renaissance painting, with enough general background to cope with the contingencies of connoisseurship in other areas. General knowledge in the decorative or graphic arts or Western sculpture is all to the good." If such curators can restrain themselves sufficiently to get on well with the exhibits staff, then taste alone should allow them to cooperate sufficiently to work out permanent and temporary exhibits that manage to please the public and the critics, at the same time keeping their trustees interested in new museum acquisitions, or lulled into a sense of satisfaction about their own collections.

I have already referred to the lack of museum employment of really expert curators in research which the problems of art galleries tend to encourage. As Eisler points out, these problems are self-perpetuating. If "experts" have to be hired to write catalogues, and if foundations will even give grants to help pay for such experts on contract, how can a hard-pressed art museum be encouraged to take on expert curatorial staff? It is easier and cheaper to employ the sort of generalized paragon described above, and leave the experts in the Art History departments of universities, or in some other city or country where they belong.

The main problem here, it seems to me, is not so much the dilettantism or hardheaded fiscal practicality of the board of trustees, which might tend to smother innovation, but rather questions of space, the groaning board provided by the collections and the lack of more table leaves on which to spread them out.

My own point of view is that art museums should start some serious rethinking of their roles, based on an assessment of community support, space, and the real meaning of museums, especially in our own convulsive age, as centers for research and education.

If an urban art museum is confined to a single *fin de siècle*

Greek revival marble palace, and for reasons of zoning or park encroachment or high cost is actually prevented from enlarging its present campus (and here I use the word campus advisedly, as a symbolic term), then there are two courses open to it: either give up the building and move elsewhere, or compromise—keep the building but move and split into another area. My own preference would be to give up and start all over again from the ground up, perhaps persuading the municipality to take over the marble splendor for an additional library or a palace of culture or perhaps even, if run by the town fathers, a palace of sport.

An art museum should consist of perhaps three large spaces. One would be for more or less permanent exhibition, but built rather inexpensively, like a high-school gymnasium, emphasizing an inconspicuous, flexibly designed series of partitions and wall surfaces inside, with, preferably, artificial lighting. Perhaps on the other side of a courtyard or sculpture area could be the "Jeu de Paume," the temporary exhibition area, again broken up into flexible multipurpose spaces, for exhibiting everything from monolithic contemporary works of our present sad days of wistfully introspective creation to period exhibits which could be shown in similarly severe areas but with a few accessories to lend *ton* and verisimilitude. Again, lighting and climate control would be stressed and various shipping-receiving facilities as well as security would be highly evolved and carefully planned.

The third large space could be designed to complement the others, and would be like a combination stacks and rare-book study area of a library. Here all the collections could be stored with maximum accessibility for scholars and conservation experts. Special study and carrell spaces should be set aside for visitors, as well as laboratories for demonstration and research. Students in this area would be confined to the graduate level or above, and public educational services would be elsewhere, perhaps in a low ambulatory-like edifice connecting this essentially library structure and the area for permanent exhibits.

The two areas for permanent or temporary exhibits, large and highly flexible, would have to be designed for the realization that present-day mass museum attendance is only just beginning. They should therefore be thought of as built in the style of World's Fair pavilions whose superstructure might be constructed on a framework or base of permanent utilities, heat, light, water, gas, climate control, and so on, in such a way that the whole exterior skin could be stripped off or changed around if new developments in twenty years made the original circulation pattern and space allocations obsolete. There is a zoo in England, the Chester Zoo, all of whose buildings are simply cocoonlike spaces, connected to utilities, so that as new techniques of maintaining, rearing and keeping animals for public exhibition are developed, the Zoo board has no hesitation in demolishing a twenty-year-old structure, created for semipermanence, in favor of the new shape or size required. This, incidentally, is excellent practice for modern architects, keeping them humble as well as intellectually on their toes in the process. No architectural dry rot or the production of self-inflating mausoleums can exist here.

In such spaces of the future, fifty or sixty thousand visitors a day might be able to come and see some figurative *Mona Lisa*, be fed and watered and flow out again. At the second level, school classes and various sorts of teaching opportunities through college age should be available in workshops or laboratory surroundings where classrooms with teaching aids could be maintained. Slides and reproductions should be available, as well as study-collection material, giving a minimal time and opportunity only to the visit to the temporary exhibit or the permanent hall. Some "touch and see" material must be included here, as this is really the sole conveyor of meaning for many young people. To handle something can make all the difference for the intensive class. My own feeling is that tours of the art galleries and lectures in them mean far less to young people than is assumed. Distractions are too many, and in general, a real live hand-painted masterpiece is far less momentous an experience for a young person than a teacher or an art-loving adult thinks. Young people today have different eating habits as well as intellectual ingesting habits than do adults. Television and snacks between meals, as well as the denigration of mealtime as a family ritual, have seen to that. Original works of art do not have the same inherent sanctity for young people. Rather, anything handmade that they can touch carries a special mystique. The possibility of learning crafts seems almost like an antique magic, and something that many people would struggle with for at least a quotient of time, as in learning to play a musical instrument. For these things are expressions of individual personality and creativity, a precious buffer against homogenization.

In this day and age, so full of the insecurity of old values and so full of the presence of organic social change, museums would do well to be as "hypersensitive to the forces at work in the contemporary world" as Germain Bazin says they are, and I do not mean merely solving the groaning-board problem of what to exhibit, what not to exhibit and how to label it all. As Bazin suggests, museums of the future may have to be more library-like, with a central storage and study area as I have suggested above for the experts, as well as special areas for education and decentralized small satellite museums for suburbia as well as, I would hope, for the rundown urban areas. Branch museums near schools in poverty areas could do much to increase those quotients of the standard of living not yet contemplated by the planners. The satellite museums could take much of the burden of overwhelming crowds away from the central institution. Museums could place their buffet tables at dispersed points throughout the community, tailoring their offerings to the tastes or appetites of the kinds of people served. Meanwhile the central complex could go back to being what an art or a science museum should be, a research institute (Bazin calls it a "cultural complex") a flexible center for studies involving the collections themselves.

CHAPTER EIGHT

Museums and the Future 3:
Art Fiddles While Rome Burns

In previous chapters I have written about my hope that artists, people who are involved in the precarious and agonizing act of putting their own ideas and their own approach to life into some sort of visual form, might be able to work in museums. This would involve entering museums and allying themselves with the age-old but often forgotten idea that a museum was a center for a "sacred band" of scholars who indeed wished to work and to put the fruit of their labors into a tangible, communicable form.

I was amused recently, looking over the original plans for the Smithsonian building of 1846, as submitted by the four competing architects—John Norman, James Renwick (the eventual winner), Isaiah Rogers and Owen Warren—to see that in one case, the proposed "art gallery" which was to occupy part of the building had next to it "three drawing rooms" for the accommodation of artists, presumably artists in residence. I was amused because of course many artists by the turn of this century and up through World War II thought of museums as morgues, and also because the present social and economic success of artists has led universities to inaugurate a spate of programs to do with artists in residence, a new version of the *thiasos*.

At present we are suffering from a crisis of confidence in what is still called art. The beginning of this century continued the reverence for masterpieces, and the conviction that genius walked on the earth, even though it could not be discerned at once. A masterwork, created by genius, spoke in a language of its own, told the truth only later. It was a monologue, like Cassandra's, not perhaps understood at once, perhaps disbelieved, but eventually triumphant over time itself. Of course, a museum was a repository for masterworks, to be conserved, as in a temple, and eventually to be worshiped, subjectively—not a religion in itself, but closely akin to a religious experience.

All this broke down somehow, though just when the date came is subject to doubt. Neither science nor wars can be said to have caused the breakdown. I agree with Clark that "in studying the history of art the interplay between scientific or intellectual trends and what I may call professional movements within the arts themselves has to be treated with great caution; and some intoxicating analogies are best resisted." [27] Quoting Kandinsky, he points out the artist's own confusion, when he apparently heard that the God-made atom had been split.

"Science," Kandinsky is quoted as saying, and thus somehow mixing up science with the laws of nature as studied by scientists, "seemed to be destroyed. Its most important basis was only a delusion, an error of the learned." Thus Kandinsky dates his decision to leave the world of reality and to branch off into abtract painting on a breakthrough in physics. He had already been painting in an abstract style prior to 1913, which was not only the date of the splitting of the atom but the year of the New York Armory Show.

Of course one could date the changeover in artists' attitudes about art and academies and museums much earlier. In the very years of the 1840s when architects were thinking of combining art in creation with art hung on the walls in the proposed Smithsonian building, the knell of academic art had already sounded. The brief imperial renaissance of David and Ingres was over, and Courbet, to be followed by Manet and many others, was ushering in the age of the impressionists, even though it might be fifty years before they began to be understood or seriously collected. The premonitory expositions of light and line by Goya, by Magnasco, and even the earlier "sketchy" flashes of color by the great masters like Hals, all contributed to the triumph of the subjective. Artists wanted to paint as *they* saw things, not as they laboriously learned their trade in an academy. The impressionists created a revolution in ways of thinking and looking at life, whether in figure painting or in landscape. Everyone to his own, looking at it in his own way, was a new and at first unaccepted concept. Perhaps there was a new sense of freedom all about. Revolution was in the air. New scientific theories abounded. The common man was in triumph temporarily, but these painters, bourgeois all, despised bourgeois values. If art was academic and taste was decreed in palaces and temples of the arts, venerating safe and solid values, then, even though royalty was dead, and revolution had triumphed, the new enemy was the solid, stolid citizen, the "square."

By the beginning of this century the newer experimental trends in art, the post-impressionist era of Cezanne and the beginnings of cubism represented by Picasso must have seemed incomprehensible to many artists at the time. In America at least, painting, while still conventional in essence, was capable of becoming highly experimental in the development of color, and in themes of social change, in its searching for honesty in depicting squalor and brutality in human life. The period of the Eight, the Ashcan School, represented highly sincere, highly motivated socially related painting as well as fine painting. Even abstract painting like that of Dove conveys a sense of great conscience.

Meanwhile, abroad, Picasso's discovery of primitive forms of art as exemplified by little known religious and magic figures of exotic cultures began a new revolution. As Picasso and his followers turned to unknown cultures, to Africa and the South-west Pacific for inspiration, a threshold was crossed which could not be reversed. The traditions of the past had included also an understanding of the roots of our history, of a sense of ordered and sequential events. Even if the past represented art forms which were to be discarded, one could not also reject entirely our own civilized past with its overtones of religious experience and faith. Any European or American artist at least knew from whence his roots derived. But no one knew the origins of African culture in those days. Still no one knows the meaning of the Easter Island figures, and very few today have any knowledge of the quintessential meaning of the fetish figures of New Ireland and the New Hebrides.

I believe that Picasso was seeking inwardly for ways to break up figures into essential blocks, and that primitive sculptures of unknown cultures afforded him an opportunity to experiment toward cubism and eventually to "abstract" his shapes into blocks or pieces of blocks or patches, which happened to interest him. I believe that he was honest in this, and that for the ensuing two generations iconologists who have been seeking to create a new worship of the so-called primitive in art, have been missing the boat. To understand the art of cultures which are strange and alien to white Caucasian art historians is a monumental task in itself. To remove the objects from their context, in association with the rest of the fabric of their lives, is to make the task almost impossible. To cap the climax, most of these cultures are already dead or dying, as I have noted earlier, over-whelmed by the rush to be modern and up-to-date, to be industrialized, and to ape the West. In many cases the art historian would have to be a medium, capable of a high degree of skill in parapsychology.

By the end of World War I the impressionists were largely safely dead, and the beginning of the monetary ascendancy of their pictures heralded their collection in museums. The twenties and thirties saw the development of important private collections and nascent public ones, largely museums of contemporary art in which could be enshrined the products of the former rebels. For better or worse, the Armory Show had galvanized American painters into realizing that there were all sorts of new movements stirring abroad and that there were dealers who could purvey controversial paintings. While the conservative dealers were still selling Gainsboroughs and Romneys to look out serenely over Georgian sideboards, the avant-garde dealers, especially in Paris, heralded a new tradition.

Parallel with the rise of post-impressionism out of impressionism after the turn of this century, there came another, separate wave of revolt, a feeling of disgust with the complacency of life and the callousness of our civilization. This was the philosophy known as dada, and its painting expression took the form of poking fun, of ridiculing the banal in life. Dada and its outgrowths, the Fauves and the surrealists, ebbed during World War I, but the surrealists came back strong in the late twenties in a mannerist technique of high realism invoked for the representation of shock themes derived from Freudian subjects, figures of belief or of disbelief, intended to convey psychological meaning. Recently, instead of merely being a stage in the evolution of aspects of cubism and surrealism, dada has come to be thought of as a precursor of a continuing movement of today, the curious triumph of non-art, of the nihilism with which so much of life is permeated at the moment. In his essay on dada, Rubin[28] points out that dada "concentrated on subverting middle-class culture," but "Surrealists . . . were more concerned with what would come after. They would replace anarchic Dada *gestes* by constructive, collective action." Instead, what happened was that surrealism has sunk into a kind of obscurity, and the ghosts of dada and its essentially nihilist outlook stride across the present in kaliedoscopic color, called "psychedelic," and, a-long with electronic music, pop, op, and other kinetic effects induced by stage and screen and video, occupy the temporary center of the stage.

This stage helps provoke the crisis. The crisis is still not un-derstood abroad, for at present much of the center, the action, is here. Malraux in a dated phrase said, "Though for the modern artist, art is not a religion, it is certainly a faith." [29] I submit that it is not a faith. If the successful art of today has strong overtones of dada, it is for other reasons than those advanced by the founders. Avant-gardism today is pacific, as Harold Rosen-berg has recently stated in a fascinating essay:[30] "The present art world is a demilitarized zone, flanked by avant-garde ghosts on one side and a changing mass culture on the other. This buffer area, immune to attack by both vanguard intransigence and philistine prejudice, contains an avant-garde public in which the alienation of the artist is muffled and which also pro-vides a market for the expansion of mass culture into more sophisticated forms."

During the period of the rise of so-called modern art during the last century, formal, traditional art became known as aca-demic art. Although romantic painters, like romantic writers, were in essence in revolt against the classical tradition, the revolt was not overt. The great landscapists like Constable could be hung in the art museum without the sense of an alarming break in continuity. In the United States great landscapists infused with romanticism like Moran and Church abounded. But roman-tic painting was not in obvious conflict with the older tradition, nor was romantic sculpture. The sculpture of this period was often suffused with sentiment, the marble positively dewy and dimply with expression, as in Canova's works. Telling a story of some sort was still predominant. Even if the story was about myths, as with Corot's nymphs, it was never abstract. Most of the Barbizon School evolved in a realist classical tradition which included absolute realist-romantics like Gérôme, celebrating a fascination with the exotic, the world of the Middle East, where harems and pashas abounded, and which influenced the urge towards "harem corner" decoration in sumptuous living rooms of the period.

Another last gasp of traditionalism was the attenuated Gothicism of Burne-Jones and the Morris school of design. This seems to have been a late Victorian fashion which sank of its own formal weight not long after its launching, seemingly lifeless and freighted with wholly dead symbolism, a house of wraiths. But the world of the academic continued long after its official death, perpetuated by art galleries, by dealers and by decorators, the purveyors of the sumptuous. If there were nudes, they were the red-haired nudes of Henner. More often there were the gold-framed "telling the story" pictures, cavaliers and cardinals, maidens and boors, a Germanic-out-of-Flemish mishmash of seventeenth-century ladies and gentlemen, painted with utmost realism by painters like Pasini and Israels, long since consigned to Atlantic City boardwalk auction palaces.

Realism seemed to die between the two World Wars. The great triumph of this genre was in mural painting, and the heroic constructions in sculpture and architecture, which emerged in a kind of neo-imperialist tradition. In Italy the Fascist regime encouraged monumental art, celebrating the pseudo-triumphs of Mussolini. Soldiers, peasants, workers, in monumental form, sprang to life in murals and sculpture in Italy, in Mexico, in the USSR celebrating the triumphs of communism, in Spain celebrating the Franco regime, in Germany, of course, and even all over the United States in WPA post-office murals. Whether Fascist, Communist or Democrat, the end result was a sterile academic realism which most of us thought had long since died, except perhaps in Russia, until we all saw in wonder and amazement the rise of the complacent neo-imperialist ghost, the Rayburn building in Washington, opened in 1965, with its triumphantly trite sculptural adornments.

Not long before World War II artists like Josef Albers, Willem de Kooning and Picasso himself began to extend themselves into the world of complete abstraction. Many younger artists, following their lead, as well as surrealists like Max Ernst, joined in what gradually built up as a new movement. Leaders among them were Arshile Gorky, Jackson Pollock, Mark Rothko and Barnett Newman. Abstraction created abstract expressionism. This was a new mood but in an accepted tradition. All the artists were draftsmen. That is they could draw. They simply chose to experiment, to "do their own thing," and to launch into a totally subjective world of their own, without let or hindrance, and without any close relation to the public or to dealers. They were in this sense avant-garde, and of course some of them expressed a sense of alienation, or boredom with the banal in everyday life, though a man like Albers (as Dove, earlier) always seemed to me essentially at peace with the world.

World War II produced a traumatic reaction, which has still not ended. The artist, like the architect, shocked out of any sense of belief or credulity in our culture by the revelations of the prison camps and the atrocities of the Nazis, thought much of death. One of my sculptor friends, numbed almost into a state of coma, could do nothing for a year or two after the war but draw emaciated, tortured bodies, decaying after death. Putrefying, the world itself seemed to deliquesce before his eyes. The abstractions of blank spaces, vast, monumental concrete walls of prisons, seemed to captivate architects, who began to create new buildings of poured, and later stressed, concrete forms, leaving the wooden impressions of the plank forms on the exterior surface for "textural" effect, or embedding pebbles or other aggregates in the concrete in a manner designed to cause skin abrasions and contusions to the unwary.

Artists continued to be pleasantly out of phase, alienated and mostly uncollected, until the early nineteen-fifties, when suddenly abstract expressionism, assemblage and pop art all began to be taken seriously. At once, contemporary artists were in vogue. They began to make money, and two or three dealers in New York and Los Angeles began to find that they were in big business. The race was on for younger artists to join in. Museums as well as collectors began buying contemporary works. In a ten-year period a vast boom in contemporary art was created, still miraculously presided over by the old master Picasso, whose monumental sculpture exhibition in 1967 in New York at the Museum of Modern Art, covering sixty years or so, was so awesome as to overwhelm most of the younger artists.

Two things have become apparent. Avant-gardism, as thought of in the case of these younger artists, has ceased to exist. The younger artists today, working out the last attenuated remains of abstract expressionism, trying to elicit a tickle out of the remnants of sensationalism open to them, are not alienated any more. They have gone commercial, along with their toothpaste tubes and soup cans. They are part of the mass culture and the mass media. So long as they are fashionable, not alienated and making money, their claws have been drawn. This is Rosenberg's "demilitarized zone," mentioned earlier.

One art critic I know suggests that this stage of contemporary interest and support of art represents the triumph of perhaps two hundred people, a cabal of artists, dealers, museum curators and perhaps a very few collectors, most of whom are likely to be the sheep who follow rather than the bellwethers. At present, way-out art, passively accepted by the public and capable of being merchandised, has itself become academic.

The second point is that the attenuation of this mode of art now prevents us from discovering whether the artists and sculptors who make galvanized metal cubes, or lean planks against walls, or suspend large sections of manila hemp rope from the wall in ultrasimplified (therefore Zen-inspired?) patterns, can actually draw or sculpt. There is no proof that they can, any more than that a contemporary dressmaker can cut a pattern, or a contemporary architect can master the intricacies of his craft, or a contemporary musician can actually play a recognized instrument. Proof is lacking in fashionable, academic creation today, and no one is able to say whether the emperor is wearing any clothes or not. That is why there is a crisis of confidence in art and art values.

Museums are placed in a curious position by all of this. Traditionally, that is to say during the past two hundred years, museums have not collected contemporary or avant-garde art. Traditionally a *galleria* did not buy art, but received known, recognized art by bequest or gift. Patrons supported artists, commissioned works, and on their death bequeathed them to museums. There was a time lapse of some sort. A time lapse helped create a consensus. Art was admired when it was known to be in the masterwork tradition, or, older in chronology, had received the accolade of considered opinion. Instant art was not collected by museums. Now instant art is made for essentially commercial purposes. Happenings are part of the world of entertainment and commerce. A museum is in a new dilemma in regard to artists. Should they reenter the *thiasos*? The sacred grove is now profaned. Art is created for dress patterns, or part of a projection for next year's fashions by the cabal. By creating museums for modern art, we have abandoned the traditional approach of art museums to art. A museum of this sort is more like a trade fair, exhibiting works made for the moment, but not given any collective value, except insofar as fashion decrees that they are "in." Formerly the value of an artist's work increased only after his death. Now we find that certain proven living artists, recognized in their lifetime, like Henry Moore or Calder, rise in value with every year, even though they are still producing. They could not produce enough to feed this market of scarcity, where there is little certainty any more, and virtually no criteria remain.

If we are to schedule exhibitions of light bulbs, of fluorescent tubing, of tiny nudes in glass boxes (remember the World's Fair peepshow nude of 1938?), then these objects should be shown in contemporary craft museums as decorative arts along with handicrafts. Let such art museums have studios or "drawing rooms" associated with them, for people to make cornshuck dolls, use hand looms, experiment with plastic materials in constructions, work as tinsmiths or in any other sort of creative craft. I submit that none of this is vanguard. Rather, it should give people a chance to work with their hands in creative crafts. They can do it for sale or not, but let them do something. There is at least a chance that such an incredible marriage between what some people call "art" and what some people call "crafts" might make sense. As the artists are no more at odds with the public, and as the public, besides being affluent, is desperately uncertain about what it wants, perhaps an unspoken craving for creation, for the therapy of working with one's hands, could be evoked by all this. Perhaps the only difficulty would be that the dealers and artists who make money out of this myth of avant-gardist art, and the critics who produce tortured rhetoric to support it, would be confounded. Handicrafts don't seem "chic" somehow. They don't smell of money either, and as money seems to be our guiding principle in fashion these days, the trend may be hard to counter.*

* The theme of contemporary art as an extension of decorative art has been suggested by the Museum of Modern Art in New York,

136

The title of this chapter refers to my feeling that much of contemporary art is indeed "fiddling while Rome burns." Artists seem to me to owe it to themselves to be honest. Much of contemporary art is not honest, but how much is impossible to say, deluged as we are with advertising techniques, with the ebb and sway of fashion. In a time of crisis, when the urban poor and the urban failures in management confound us, when the face of America is being smothered by heaps and ribbons of cement, and a pall of smoke hangs over it all, must art consist of enigmatic nothingness or "thinginess"?

The avant-garde of today seem to me to be the realists. They are not popular with the creators of taste, therefore they must

---

which since the years of the beginning of World War II has exhibited contemporary crafts and design. The emphasis has of course been essentially on the best of modern industrial design from coffeepots to womb chairs. This is still a far cry from arts and crafts which emphasize handiwork skills, or industrial design as may be seen today at the new Museum of Contemporary Crafts. Handicraft traditions having to a large extent been obviated by the very nature of technology and mechanization today; there is suddenly a new outburst of industrial design using modern materials like plastics. The effect is stunning as well as competent and inventive, and serves to leave studio artists somewhat in the lurch.

In an effort to abandon realism and plumb the wells of abstraction, many modern artists have fallen between two stools today. They have lost sight of aspects of realism which would prove them masters of their atelier craft. At the same time they have failed to keep up to the assured brilliance of some of the free and avowedly businesslike styles of Famery and other industrial designers working in plastics without the inhibitions or the illusions of calling themselves creative "artists" as such. Artists are in danger of being merely dabblers today, amateurs in new materials, and at the same time no longer masters of their classic medium.

represent a vanguard movement. Many of them are so good that they manage to survive even in art circles, as does the sculptor Manzu, for example. The paintings of Wyeth are nostalgic, evocative of moods of long ago. They are immensely popular but not perhaps in the vanguard. They belong in an art gallery. But there are other realist artists, younger ones who are coming along and will, I think, represent where art is going. Let architecture also follow, if you please. We have had a surfeit of sugar cubes laid on end, with faceless honeycomb windows row on row. Let there be some real texture for a change and some real variety, else architecture is surely dead.

Life is a tapestry, a Bayeux tapestry, or a makimono scroll, unrolling as we go with endless combinations and rich permutations. As Haskins recently remarked:

> No characteristic of the computer that suggests the action of the brain has been developed more dramatically in recent years than its "memory." . . . Perhaps it is this spectacular advance in the memory capabilities of computers that has particularly fostered the idea that machines thus endowed . . . could by their operations shed some light on the specific nature of human recollection.
>
> Such an analogy, however, must be regarded with reserve. . . . For the brain and the computer, in last analysis, are very different things. [The brain shows] a structural and functional complexity unexampled elsewhere in the living world, except perhaps among the great conurbations of our time. And since even in the greatest urban centers we do not yet deal with individual aggregates of citizens numbering ten billion or more, while the human brain does include approximately that number of individual neurons in its compass, the brain may well be the most staggeringly complex biological organization in the world.[31]

Human life is made even more precious by the thought that the human brain is more intricately various than anything yet seen on earth. Surely, then, the arts have an obligation to take part in reaffirming the value of that life. The new museum cannot be any more passive than the artist. It should be a center for actions and what someone has recently termed "trans-actions." Knowing the past, at home with the present, the museum should be able to project the future, and in this the artist should be compelled to play his part.

CHAPTER NINE

Some Impressions of My Own

My own philosophy of museums became established at the age of ten one winter when we were living in Paris. One of the advantages of playing in the Tuileries Gardens as a child was that at any one moment one could be riding the carrousel, hoping against hope to catch the ring. The next instant one might be off wandering the paths among the chestnuts and the plane trees, looking for the old woman who sold *gaufres*, those wonderful hot wafer-thin, wafflelike creations dusted over with powdered sugar. A third instant in time, and there was the Punch and Judy show, mirror of life, now comic, now sad. Another moment and one could wander into one of the galleries at the Louvre. I still remember the day I found the ship models, fantastically intricate in skeletal form, or cut away to show interiors, high-pooped galleons, eighteenth-century men of war, or the early-nineteenth-century marriage of technologies of sail and steam. Then out to the garden again where there was a patch of sand in a corner to build sand castles. Then back to the Louvre to wander through the Grand Gallery.

There was no essential difference in all this. The juxtaposition was natural and easy. No threshold of tiredness and lack of concentration was reached. It was as easy as breathing in and out. For children, then, museums should be infinitely easy, diverse, varied. There should be fun and games somewhere, perhaps just outside, and concentration and indirect learning inside, but there should be no real distinction between the two. The outside should flow into the inside, the inside out.*

Even at this age I loved sculpture and painting with an unformed eye. I adored pretty and touching little girls like Houdon's bust of Louise Broguiart, full of innocence and charm and a poignant, pensive expression. I loved stylish pictures like the Raphael portrait of Baldassare Castiglione, elegant but conveying great charm in the sitter. I used to look at military pictures, Gericault and Delacroix, for already I was buying toy soldiers, hoping some day to be able to afford Napoleon's General Staff.

My tastes ran to the saccharine sometimes. I was secretly in love with the ladies of Greuze, particularly the girl of *La Cruche Cassée*. In any case I roamed unhindered through the galleries absorbing tapestries, medieval enamel, crystal beakers, vast paintings of Marie de'Medici and her time, all in one breath.

Other days we would take my sailboat and sail it in the Luxembourg Gardens, or shop for toy soldiers, or armor and arms along the Quai du Louvre. Here, near the seed store of the Vilmorin family, there were pet shops which offered everything from soft-bills like Cuban solitaires to white mice. The arms and armor at this stage occupied me a great deal. I was taking fencing lessons and longed for a court rapier or a Scottish basket-hilted claymore, for I was very proud of my mother's Highland blood. I was heavily in thrall to Sir Walter Scott, whose endless narratives suited the spirit of derring-do engendered by the Salle Gardère and my sisters' and my fencing.

* In this connection I think that I always missed touching things when I could not do so in museums. Perhaps that is why I ran in and out so much at the Louvre. I had been to Mme. Montessori's kindergarten class in New York, and I have ever since been a firm believer in creative learning experiences and their relation to the eventual development of cognitive skills.

But it was on the way to sailboat sailing in the Luxembourg Gardens that I met the Musée de Cluny. This rapidly became my favorite museum in Paris. Here in this dark, rather dank late-fifteenth-century palace I became fascinated by the reality of history. The everyday objects of life enthralled me, from the magnificent paneling and tapestries of palace life to the clothes, particularly boots—vast postilions' boots, cavaliers' boots, ladies' boots and shoes with exaggerated toes, sometimes so long that the tip was brought up and fastened to a garter; there were the platform clogs worn to avoid filth in the streets. There were also coaches and models of coaches and incredible arms and armor including a helmet from the field of Agincourt. There were things one could touch, thank heavens. The thrill that was conveyed in touching rusty armor or horse caparisons that had once enclosed panting steeds pulling coaches over rutted cobblestones was a never-ending one. The tapestries and stained glass with their brilliant colors evoked the liveliness of the scenes in my imagination. The vault of the chapel ceiling seemed even more miraculous than those of La Sainte Chapelle. The marvelous unicorn tapestries started me off on speculations about unicorn horns, narwhal horn cups, bezoar stones, rhinoceros-horn libation wine vessels and similar legendary utensils, an interest which has never quite disappeared. I was fascinated by the quaint and sometimes grotesque shapes of aquamaniles, and I loved the fireplace with the spits. What had happened to the little turnspit dogs? Someone should have produced a turnspit dog, a little miscellaneous terrier, just to turn the spit in the Cluny Museum.

Our second city of that winter was Florence. Here we stayed long enough to infect me with a never-to-be-forgotten impression of the Uffizi and Pitti Galleries and the Bargello. Smells were very important to me and still are: wet asphalt in Paris, old harness oil, lemon oil, damp wood and stone in the Cluny, and lots of dry musty smells in Florence, mixed with the aromatic but dry-dusty smells of winter in Fiesole, bay leaves, and olive leaves, and dried-out hay. Of course, in the nineteen-twenties horses were everywhere, pulling drays and wagons, fiacres and victorias, in Paris and the Italian cities. One misses the delicious stable smells these days as a usual accompaniment of streets and museum entrances and cathedral squares where the sweepers were forever shoveling up fresh manure. Horse manure is as much a part of my memories of Florence as the cold stone and old wood, the incense smell of the churches and the damp wood, oil-leather smell of the *gallerias*.

Of the two I liked the Uffizi better, with its painted corridors. The paintings that interested me varied from the antics of the Percheron horses in battle of Paolo Uccello to the portraits, especially the rather austere profile styles of Piero della Francesca, Pollaiuolo, and the stylish, rather lush textures of Bronzino. The landscapes of Mantegna fascinated me, and like all children, I suppose, I was intensely interested in the tiny figures winding up roads to castles or in the distant village in the allegorical paintings of Piero di Cosimo and Leonardo. I bought a little box with a reproduction of Andrea del Sarto's St. John the Baptist, and also a marble copy of Donatello's St. George. Martyrdoms didn't appeal to me, and I think I was too young for nudes.

My next most vivid impressions were of Schönbrunn, for we spent a month in Vienna. To me it was curious to return not long ago to Schönbrunn, after forty years, and to see again with a start of recognition the blue-and-white Chinese porcelains in the Chinese room of that palace, to recognize them, along with the Indian miniature paintings in the "Millions" rooms which had so moved me as a child. Why I liked blue-and-white porcelain is perhaps explained by growing up with a good deal of it in our house in Connecticut, some collected by my grandfather and some by my great-grandparents. It perhaps seemed familiar,

but I know I have always liked it. The palace museum at Schönbrunn was made complete by the zoo, the oldest in Europe, with
its beautiful baroque buildings in the park. Tea in the breakfast
pavilion with elephants in the distance was a perfect foil to the
intricate scenes of war and hunting in the Mughal paintings
inset in the walls in baroque frames in that superb room in the
palace.

Several years later, when I was thirteen, we were in India
and I had my first chance to buy a Rajput painting of the Mughal period, an eighteenth-century portrait. It took three days,
and by dint of using my newfound Hindi to bargain in the manner I had read about in Kipling I got the portrait miniature for
about five dollars. Of course I was immensely proud. The possibility of visiting the Lahore Museum and seeing the great gun,
Zamzama, on its carriage outside the front of the Museum was a
dazzling one. Sure enough there it was; "a gun terrible as a
dragon and huge as a mountain," the great fourteen-foot giant
of copper and brass on which Kim had insolently lolled in the
opening scene of my favorite book on India. We saw Zamzama
in all its glory, though I could only imagine that Kim himself
was somehow personified in the urchins playing about the
Anarkali Sadr Bazaar opposite.

Lahore was the gateway to knowledge of the Greco-Buddhist
sculptures and terra-cottas of the period after Alexander the
Great's memorable conquests of the third century B.C. For some
reason unknown to me now, I was keenly interested in the
Gandhara period and persuaded my family to visit Taxila with
Sir John Marshall's guidebook in hand, although it was some
years later, at Yale, that I took Rostovtzeff's course and set about
writing a term paper on the Greco-Buddhist period.

It was this trip to India which seemed to bring out a confirmed
interest in natural history. For a while I had been leaning towards archaeology, but in the preceding winter, visits to the

Boston and the New York Museums of Natural History, and of course the New York zoos in Central Park and the Bronx, had gradually begun to leave their mark. I had become well-inoculated with the virus of natural history exhibits by the curious verisimilitude of the diorama of the beaver and its underwater den in the Boston Museum of Natural History. The oily yellow surface water feeling conveyed by the smooth glass seemed perfect to me, as did the modeled cow lilies and the underwater world cut away below at which I peered. It could not have been more real to me than if I had been one of Charles Kingsley's water babies.

In New York, Louis Agassiz Fuertes' paintings of the flamingos of Andros Island, with the foreground designed by Dr. Frank Chapman, seemed completely real. Shimmering in the sun, the vermilion flamingos transported me to a tropic isle in a way I found irresistible. And so it was that when we came to India in that winter of 1926–7, I was fully prepared for a bout of museum-going. Having arrived at the port of Bombay, my family naturally made directly for the Prince of Wales Museum which since 1923 had housed the exhibits of the Bombay Natural History Society. I realized later that natural history museums in the Oriental region have largely originated as private collections or as a result of the efforts of private societies such as the Bombay Natural History Society, which had been founded in 1883 by a group of amateur naturalists in business and career government service in India. The Prince of Wales Museum is an impressive structure in a distinctive beturreted version of Victorian-Mughal style. It now includes a later wing, opened in 1939, full of natural history dioramas, the most modern of their kind in Asia. But we were too early for these modern groups, which I did not see till World War II. However, there was a splendid exhibit of great Indian hornbills at the nest, the tree cut away to show the temporarily incarcerated mother and young walled up with mud and dung in true-to-life form so that the nest aperture is only a slit through which the male passes in food to his charges. The stuffed male was William, formerly a pampered pet of the Society, who had lived in the Society's exhibit rooms for twenty-six years until he died, and who had presumably never had occasion to perform such arduous domestic chores in life. During his lifetime William was death on vermin, which are always plentiful in office and museum buildings in Bombay. As the Society reported much later in their *History* in 1933, "Cockroaches were to his liking, and a mouse, a snake or even a large rat he dearly loved. . . . One rat he held in his pickaxe beak for more than an hour before finally crunching it up. If he had not overeaten himself on a bit of wire he would probably be alive to this day. Others have succeeded him, but the 'Office Canary,' as he was affectionately called, is greatly missed."

I was sorry to see William merely stuffed, but there were two live pythons, one fifteen feet long, the other twelve. That is, there had been just before we got there, but the larger, roused by the fact that his companion had happened to make away with a black partridge, ended by swallowing the partridge (which was in his former friend at the time) plus a small red blanket, so that there happened to be only one visible python left.

From Bombay we went to Calcutta where perhaps the largest museum in Asia exists—the Indian Museum, founded in 1866, and based on the collections of the private society, the Asiatic Society of Bengal. That earlier museum, I discovered, had received its real impetus from the East India Company's Board of Directors, who, in 1814, had appointed Dr. Nathaniel Wallich curator of archaeological and zoological collections. Wallich and his successors, notably Edward Blyth, had presided over the amassing of important collections through the nineteenth century made by amateur naturalists, men in the police, customs and forestry services, as well as naturalists attached to various military, punitive or boundary expeditions. Marine collections were made by surgeon-naturalists, so-called, aboard R.I.M. survey steamer *Investigator*. There were important exhibit galleries in those days of insects, fish, amphibia, reptiles, birds and mammals, and I joined huge milling throngs of Indians in fascinated appraisal of the stuffed animals. Most of these stuffed creatures were very well mounted, as taxidermy was thriving in India in prewar days due to the lively competition among the maharajas and other wealthy big-game fanciers to bedeck their walls with grimacing creatures of the jungle.

Southern and eastern Asia have somehow come to be a second home to me from those early impressions of mine on the 1926 trip down to the present. I have been visiting museum collections there and working with their curators since 1939. Many of these institutions, formerly in the so-called Indian Native States, have in postwar years simply foundered in the cause of democracy. Others perhaps just quietly became extinct like the municipal museum of Fyzabad full of stuffed wild dogs and hyenas of which our British guide remarked decisively that "the taxidermy is deplorable."

Since becoming a professional biologist and having made so many subsequent visits to India, I have gotten to know many of these museums from the inside as well as out. The Bombay Natural History Society continues today to be a flourishing research institution with a published journal, scientific collections and modern exhibits in the Prince of Wales Museum. The study collections number in the thousands: 20,400 birds, 17,000 mammals, 6,000 snakes, 60,000 insects including types of Indian and southwest Asian species.

These collections survived World War II undisturbed, in contrast to those of the Indian Museum. As they were under threat of Japanese attack, the valuable research materials in zoology at Calcutta were evacuated to a stately house in Benares

147

called Kaiser Castle belonging to Kaiser Sham Shere Jang Baha-
dur Rana of Nepal. The Ganges River rose disastrously in 1942
putting nine feet of water into the rooms of Kaiser Castle. When
I dropped off in Benares, during the War in 1943 to see the
types and other valuable specimens many of the small bird
specimens resembled miniature cheroots, tightly compacted,
mummified objects covered with a thin cylinder of Ganges silt
or else just skin, all the feathers drifting about in small heaps
in the boxes. Tragic and disheartening as this was, the museum
has since been making valiant efforts to reassemble the research
collections in Calcutta and gradually to bring the exhibits up to
date. Especially in the field of paleontology, important efforts
have been made to resume field research in the Siwalik beds of
northwest India, one of the best areas of the world for research
in fossils of the late Cenozoic, especially the Pliocene and
Pleistocene. Paleontology has even sparked a new museum in
India, this one at Chandigarh, in East Punjab, at the new university celebrated for its Le Corbusier architecture as well as
its fine faculty.

Ceylon has several national museums. The most important is
the Colombo Museum, which I first visited in 1939. The stucco
building, Georgian in feeling, with columns here and there, sits
in the middle of a small park in a traffic circle à la Washington,
fiercely bright in the noonday sun, humid and panting at dusk
and dawn, for that is Colombo. Even the flamboyants and
jacarandas and the mountainous thunderhead clouds tinged
with pinkish yellow fail to dispel the constant hothouse feeling.
World War II dealt the museum a heavy blow, as the exhibit
cases were requisitioned by the military authorities for reasons
which seem mysterious in retrospect; the cases were returned
in 1946, largely broken and useless. By 1943 the building was
full of staff and khaki-clad bureaucrats, and rolls of barbed wire
lay half-uncoiled here and there as an afterthought. The exhibits

had all been stored elsewhere along with the research collections for fear of bombing, and as so often happens, moving and storage proved to be incredibly more damaging than a bomb would have been. Now restored, the museum still has impressive collections in anthropology, paleontology and mineralogy, and representative collections of animals, some 65,000 insects, 20,000 marine invertebrates and over 5,000 fish (estimated). There are perhaps 2,000 birds and a number of mammals, including a few types. The retired director, Dr. Paul E. Pieris Deraniyagala, who was kind to me during the war, holds a Cambridge "blue" in boxing and is particularly interested in paleontology, having collected as far afield as the Fayum beds in Egypt.

There are three remaining museums which I have come to know in Southeast Asia. The Raffles Museum in Singapore is perhaps the largest. Founded in 1844, it is named after that Orlando-like figure, Sir Stamford Raffles, who was Governor of Malacca, then of Java for the East India Company following various political rearrangements at the time of the Napoleonic Wars, and who concerned himself in government and Oriental politics, law, art, architecture, ethnography, entomology and zoology—to name a few of his specialties. The museum has large collections in zoology and ethnography, and was presided over, when I first visited it in 1938, by a delightful and learned man, Frederick N. Chasen (who disappeared in a small boat like so many others in early 1942 during the evacuation of the city and its invasion by Japanese troops). I was amazed to see displayed there an enormous mounted hamadryad or king cobra, said to be some 22 or 23 feet long, wriggling its majestic girth the length of a massive glass case. Any such length outdistances by far the world's record. Chasen later admitted during a prolonged dinner in a Chinese restaurant that the skin of a freshly skinned snake may prove to have rather elastic properties if judiciously handled by a taxidermist.

Burma has no natural history museum, perhaps because of its Buddhist tradition, nor has Thailand, though my friend Nai Boonsong Lekagul is valiantly fighting for one and presides in an honorary capacity over some dioramas and exhibits at Chulalongkorn University. UNESCO recently gave help to Thailand's proposed museum project by sending Dr. J. W. Evans, Director of the Australian Museum of Sydney, to Bangkok for two museum missions in 1962, and again in 1964. An area of 4.5 acres has been set aside for the purpose in the compound of Chulalongkorn University and all that remains now is for the government of Thailand to find perhaps a million dollars (U.S.) for a first five-year budget program. It is to be hoped that the government will do something positive, for a natural history museum could add greatly to the cultural attractions of Bangkok, and exhibits would stimulate a much-needed interest in conservation. Wild animal species, especially the large showy ones, are disappearing from Thailand at a rate parallel to Thailand's indigenous culture. Soon there will be just museums, zoos and exhibits of folk culture for the tourist to see, let alone the inhabitants, who in the new affluence will become tourists in their own country.

The Sarawak Museum in Borneo was founded in 1844 under the patronage of the Brooke family, the famous "white Rajahs." It specializes in ethnology, essentially of the Dayak and related tribes, in archaeology and prehistory including exhibits of the famous Niah caves, and in local zoology, especially birds. The museum publishes an important "Journal." There are also significant collections of ceramics, beads, metal and other objects dating back more than 1,500 years from the beginning of trade with mainland China. The former curator, the energetic Tom Harrisson, who with his anthropologist wife, Barbara, has now emigrated to Cornell University, worked like a beaver after World War II to revitalize and bring up to date the old museum and museum activities in Sarawak and nearby territories. Their efforts represent one of the most valued forms of educational give-and-take between white Westerners and aboriginal tribes in an area of the world where such contacts today are so fragile and tenuous, so steeped in the tensions of the current wave of anticolonialism and racial propaganda. The future just may be a little less hazardous because of their efforts. A recent valuable summary of their research program is "History, Science, the Arts and Nature in Sarawak" (1961–1962), a reprint from the *Annual Report* of Sarawak, available from the museum in Kuching. One of Tom Harrisson's triumphs was participating in the rediscovery of *Lanthanotus borneensis*, perhaps the rarest lizard in the world, a sluggish "missing link" species the size of a small skink, which lives in damp leafmold along lowland riverbanks, an enviable niche, surely.

Indonesia has a celebrated natural history museum. The famous Buitenzorg botanical gardens spread lushly all about several square stone buildings which house research laboratories, greenhouses, a library and a museum. Founded in 1894 under Dr. Melchior Treub, the great botanist, the gardens and laboratories were part of a flourishing research activity in the East Indies, developed first by the Dutch Company of the Indies, later by the Dutch government. Here World War II not only convulsed the politics and economics of the great chain of islands in Indonesia but dealt a body blow to pure research. Rechristened Bogor after independence, Buitenzorg and its museum and allied institutions continue to look much the same as before. The museum, however, is in difficulties. There are important collections here in entomology, marine and vertebrate zoology, as well as a herbarium, and of course a fine library and a bulletin series, "Treubia." But staff is all but nonexistent.

When I was there last, in 1954, I drove up to the Bogor laboratories with the head of the UNESCO mission in Java, a refugee professor from Eastern Europe, and a newly arrived American, head of a branch of a large United States foundation. As we walked about the thirty-year-old laboratories our American friend suddenly threw out his hand with an expansive gesture and said, "Isn't it wonderful to see all the things this new progressive Indonesian government has done—and when you think back to the old days of reactionary colonialism." My UNESCO professor friend and I exchanged amused glances.

Recently I have been in touch with the new head of the natural and applied science activities of the Indonesian government. His attitude towards museums and conservation is greatly encouraging. Perhaps his new government, now seeking counsel in the West, will help him, and we in our turn can help and thus insure that the future will be less precarious than the immediate past.

To the northeast of Indonesia there are the National Museum of the Philippines, largely destroyed during World War II and not actively under redevelopment, and the Museum of Hong Kong, demolished when the City Hall was torn down in 1933 and its contents stored since then at the University. In Taipei, Taiwan, there is a museum which has considerable collections in vertebrate zoology and which issues publications, and of course the new fine arts museum which I have not yet seen.

In Shanghai there were formerly zoological collections at Sikawei Museum and the Asiatic Society, but I do not know what happened to them. Several museums of art and folk art were mentioned in Basil Gary's article in *Museum*, the UNESCO periodical, in 1958 (vol. 2).

In Japan, my favorite of many museums is the only museum in that country wholly devoted to ornithology. It is the center for Japan's ornithological research. It was founded in 1910 by Marquis Yoshimaro Yamashina (as he then was called); its present building was constructed in 1931 and remained standing when his own house was destroyed in the fire raids of 1945. It is the last of the old private museums maintained by amateurs of the sciences. On my first visit to Tokyo in 1939 there were more than five such museums, and I made a progression among the great houses and museums of Prince Taka-Tsukasa, Marquis Yamashina, Marquis Kuroda, Marquess Hachisuka and Mr. Momiyama—all that I managed to see that year. Most were destroyed in the war, but the Yamashina Museum, strengthened by the support of friends and societies such as the Ornithological Society of Japan and the Japanese Association for Bird Preservation, continues to this day. Dr. Yamashina, assisted by a staff of four, including Dr. Nagahisa Kuroda, son of the former Marquis, Dr. Nagamichi Kuroda, curates a collection of over 55,000 bird and egg specimens as well as mammals and lepidoptera. There is a fine library and the museum publishes *Miscellaneous Reports*. I have a letter of recent date from Mr. Azuma, one of Dr. Yamashina's friends, which contains the familiar plaint of those who are active in the Elysian fields of museums. "Comparing with ever increasing animated activities of recent years, the present structure of the Yamashina Institute is now in a state of utterly inconvenience in many ways, too small and cramped, insufficient in room and space, so that the enlargement of the building is eagerly desired as a matter of urgent necessity."

It is indeed too bad that not all the museums are burgeoning in this way. An overcrowded museum is a healthy museum. As Mr. Markham wrote in his book on Indian museums, as I noted earlier, it was a tragedy that a nation with one sixth of the world's population has only one hundred and five museums. What is inconceivable to me is that this whole vast Oriental region with its huge share of the world's population, is an area where education is an almost hopeless task, consuming the thought and energies of national governments, the United

Nations, the Colombo Plan countries, SEATO, and the United States through grants and surplus programs, as well as our own great foundations—all of which involves us in endless plans and programs for aid. And yet in all this complex of planning and earnest good intentions, no real effort is being given to the vast educational potential of museums. From childhood on, from illiteracy up, museum education is one of the easiest and most dramatic ways to capture the human imagination. I am as sure of this as I was when I first met William the hornbill, the "office canary" in the Natural History gallery in Bombay a few years ago.

POSTLUDE

The preceding pages have been an attempt on my part to delineate what museums are and how they happened. To me they represent a setting in which little-understood, intangible things occur which have to do with stretching the minds of people. If they thus represent a force for education, it is sad to consider that the formal organizations responsible for education do not think so and fail to use museums properly, or think of them as partners in the process. One of the reasons may be an uncharitable one; schools and educators are clubbable, they have forms of union cards. Museums are rather like libraries of a generation ago. Educators then thought of those as step-relatives, purely ancillary to the processes of education. No one really helped libraries until they learned how to help themselves.

Another reason may be that museums engender a kind of awareness which leads to a sense of pleasure, of enjoyment. Pleasure and enjoyment, indeed, a sense of keen delight, or even joy, all these components of learning are not associated with education. Education is a serious business. Look how many people are involved and how many billions of dollars it costs. It can't be fun! Fun is *fun*. Education is solemn and serious. At least "training" and the transfer of accumulated facts is solemn work. Even if the latter exercises are not really education, they are assumed to be education by most people, and that's where the money goes. No wonder then that most museums are starving, drying up on the vine.

Museums are hideously understaffed and underfinanced today. They cannot possibly cope with the increasing demands placed upon them by everyone, from the public to the school systems to scholars. The bland assumption by everyone at all these levels that museums are free, that they have time and money to give out effort for every query, for every service required, is perhaps also associated with the idea of pleasure and enjoyment. If people who work in museums manage to have a good time, if they are doing what they want to do at starvation wages, then somehow there's a secret cache of money, of support somewhere. They can't be poor and be having fun! The two don't go together, at least in America. So the theme runs.

Someday Americans will wake up and discover that it isn't so. Either the museums will fold and close their doors, like the poor old mistreated railroads, or someone will have sense enough to realize that real education is fun, and that the museums' sort of education has to be paid for, just like all the other kinds. May that day be soon.

NOTES

1. Henry T. Rowell, "A Home for the Muses," *Archaeology* Vol. 19, No. 2 (1966), p. 79.
2. Alma S. Wittlin, *The Museum, Its History, and Its Tasks in Education* (London, Routledge & Kegan Paul Ltd., 1949), p. 6.
3. Francis Henry Taylor, *Babel's Tower, The Dilemma of the Modern Museum* (New York, Columbia University Press, 1945), p. 8.
4. Collections and the craze for amassing objects swept Europe in the eighteenth century, coinciding with the rise of dealers and especially auction sales; see Germain Bazin, *The Museum Age* (New York, Universe Books, Inc., 1967), Chap. 6 *et seq.*
5. T. Greenwood, *Museums and Art Galleries* (London, 1888).
6. T. Barbour, 1943 *Naturalist at Large* (Boston, Little, Brown & Co., 1943), Chap. 3, p. 168.
7. Clifford K. Shipton, "The Museum of the American Antiquarian Society," chap. in *A Cabinet of Curiosities* (Charlottesville, Va., Univ. Press of Virginia, 1967).
8. Paul H. Oehser, *Sons of Science* (New York, H. Schuman, 1949).
9. Geoffrey Hellman, *The Smithsonian, Octopus on the Mall* (New York, J. B. Lippincott, 1967).
10. Joseph Henry, *Tenth Annual Report of the Board of Regents of the Smithsonian Institution* (Washington, 1856).
11. Laurence Vail Coleman, *The Museum in America*, 3 vols. (Washington, The American Association of Museums, 1939), Vol. 2, p. 222.
12. Cyrus Adler, in *The Smithsonian Institution*, G. B. Goode, ed. (Washington, 1897), p. 290.
13. Joseph Henry, *Annual Report of the Smithsonian Institution for 1850*, quoted in W. E. Washburn, chap. in *A*

Cabinet of Curiosities (Charlottesville, Va., Univ. Press of Virginia, 1967).

14. J. B. Conant, "The Advancement of Knowledge in the United States in the Nineteenth Century," *Colorado Quarterly*, Vol. 11 (1963).
15. César Graña, "The Private Lives of Public Museums," *Trans-Action* (April 1967), pp. 20–25.
16. Taken from "The Educational Museum of the St. Louis Public Schools," *Museum Work*, Vol. 1 (6) (March 1919), pp. 163–4.
17. Albert E. Parr, "Museums of Nature and Man," *The Museum Journal*, 50 (Nov. 1950), p. 169.
18. George Kubler, *The Shape of Time* (New Haven, Yale University Press, 1962), in Chaps. 1 and 4, pp. 16, 107, 112.
19. G. E. Hutchinson, "The Naturalist as Art Critic," in *The Ecological Theater and the Evolutionary Play* (New Haven, Yale University Press, 1965).
20. Reported in "Museum News," *Journal of the American Association of Museums*, Vol. 46, No. 7 (March, 1968), pp. 11–18.
21. Herbert Friedmann, "The Significance of the Unimportant in Studies of Nature and of Art," *Proc. Amer.*

Philosophical Soc. 110, No. 4, (August 1966).
22. Harold D. Lasswell, "Strategies of Inquiry," in Daniel Lerner, ed., *The Human Meaning of the Social Sciences* (New York, Meridian Books, Inc., 1959).
23. "Torrey Canyon," J. E. Smith, ed., *Pollution and Marine Life* (London, Cambridge University Press, 1967).
24. Stephan F. de Borhegyi and Irene A. Hanson, eds., *The Museum Visitor: Selected Essays and Surveys of Visitor Reaction to Exhibits in the Milwaukee Public Museum*, Publications in Museology 3, 1968, Milwaukee Public Museum.
25. T. A. Hume, in *The Role of Museums in Education*, UNESCO Seminar, Australian Museum, Sydney, 1966.
26. Colin Eisler, "Curatorial Training for Today's Art Museum," *Curator*, Vol. 9, No. 1 (New York, 1966), pp. 51–61.
27. Sir Kenneth M. Clark, "The Value of Art in an Expanding World," in Smithsonian Institution, eds., *Knowledge Among Men* (New York, Simon and Schuster, in cooperation with the Smithsonian Institution, 1966), Chap. 3.
28. William S. Rubin, *Dada,*

Surrealism and Their Heritage (New York, The Museum of Modern Art, 1968), p. 15.

29. André Malraux, *The Psychology of Art: The Creative Act*, Vol. 2 (Princeton, N. J., Bollingen, 1949).

30. Harold Rosenberg, "The Art World; D/M/Z/ Vanguardism," in *The New Yorker* (Sept. 28, 1968).

31. Caryl P. Haskins, *Report of the President, 1966–67* (Carnegie Institution of Washington, 1968), p. 15.